SEASONS
TO SHARE

JACQUELINE ALWILL

SEASONS TO SHARE

Nourishing family &
friends with nutritious,
seasonal wholefoods

MURDOCH BOOKS
SYDNEY · LONDON

contents

introduction

I've had a passionate interest in eating and learning about food since I was little. My earliest memories are of my family's home in Sydney's Northern Beaches where our kitchen had an incredible view overlooking a nature reserve that stretched out towards the ocean. Meals of good, wholesome food were always eaten at the table over conversation. There was an island bench on our cork floor and I would climb to the edge of that to watch my parents as they prepped and cooked for my two older sisters and me. When the weekend rolled around we would have picnics down at the beach, eat fish and chips or have barbecues on our deck. We didn't rush through meals; they were a time to soak up all the nourishment that was in the food and also within our family. These moments form my early memories.

When I was ten, our family moved to Japan, and I remember experiencing complete culture shock, something I could never have been prepared for at such a young age. I didn't speak the language and arrived knowing no-one outside my own family. But our Japanese community welcomed me and taught me about their culture through food. I'd ride my bike to school each day and in the afternoon go to the shops in Hiroo to pick up a snack or some groceries for dinner. As I shopped, the grocer would teach me to count in Japanese using pieces of fruit; the sushi chef would chat to me as he sliced — ever so gracefully — through his rolls of sushi. When we went to restaurants as a family, the waiter would turn to me, the youngest in the group, and ask for our order with encouraging warmth. These were moments of learning.

APPRECIATE EVERY MOMENT ... NEVER LOSE SIGHT OF A DREAM BECAUSE OF THE UNPLANNED.

———

As a teenager back in Sydney, I immersed myself in the intricacies of food. I kept scrapbooks of recipes and articles, and I spent weekends baking and packing goodies into brown paper bags to give to friends and neighbours. I had a burning desire to be a part of the world of food, though I hadn't yet figured out what that might look like. It wasn't a time in my life where my relationship with food was always positive; I became obsessive about what I ate and this obsession dictated the way I treated myself for many years. Thankfully I overcame those problems and learned from them. I look back on that period now and feel grateful because once I'd come through that dark time, I started to dream, to create and find ways to fall in love with food again, only this time in the right way, and sharing that joy with others became my passion.

My early twenties were spent travelling abroad. I lived in a small apartment in the heart of Italy's gastronomic capital, Bologna, with three crazy, beautiful Italian girls. I struggled initially with the language barrier but we found common ground in the kitchen, where we drank €2 bottles of red wine, tore apart balls of soft burrata, peeled the most delicious prosciutto from the wax paper of our market grocer and created our own little family away from home. There was laughter, there was warmth and there was joy in simplicity. I learned about the importance of buying good-quality produce without anything else added, and this became a way of everyday life for me.

By 26, I was working as a personal trainer and was mid-way through my studies in nutritional medicine — something I'd left a career in the corporate world to do. I knew with nutrition as my foundation I would always be able to share health and happiness with people I loved — I was following my passion at last. It was during this time that the most wonderful gift came to me: the divine little human that is my son, Jet. Becoming Jet's mum has been the greatest journey of change, growth, learning, patience, fun and love. Motherhood makes me search for the best in myself, helps me appreciate every moment, pushes me to nurture not only others but also myself. It also reminds me to never lose sight of a dream because of the unplanned.

Through my love of food I have met wonderful people, shared their cultures, laughed, made mistakes, travelled and found myself on new and unexpected paths. And now it's time to share what I've learned with you. This book represents the start of new things to come, and I hope the recipes and ideas here give that sense of renewal and optimism to each person who reads it.

What I have tried to do is find a way for you to create beautiful, wholesome memories by celebrating food with the people in your life, all year round. The ingredients, textures and flavours I've chosen highlight the best each season has to offer, and the occasions are ones I've dreamt up, then gone on to bring to life and share with the people special to me. I hope what you'll discover as you cook and plan your way through some of these events is a warmth inside you as you prepare food for people you love. I hope you can take that warmth to the party, the table, the garden, the backyard fire or the picnic blanket. As you look around at the event you've created and the people you've brought together, I hope there's a proud smile on your face. That sense of 'I made this.' These little moments are what life is all about: building memories that last forever. Make this your season to share.

in my kitchen

Nutritious, wholesome and simple cooking starts with a
well-stocked kitchen. Only then do you have the resources
to draw upon as you explore your creativity. With more people
becoming interested in healthier eating and cooking from
scratch, ingredients once considered niche or hard to come
by are becoming more mainstream and widely accessible.
If there is something here that you haven't heard of or haven't
tried, I encourage you to buy that new ingredient with the
aim of using it in a few ways; note down the hits and misses
so you find ways to successfully integrate it into your diet.

ORANGE AND ALMOND CAKE
recipe page 220

in the pantry

This is by no means an exhaustive list, but the ingredients below are on constant rotation in my pantry. They are the things I couldn't get through the week without.

FLOURS AND RAISING AGENTS

For nutritional and flavour reasons, I tend to cook and bake with flours that are low-inflammatory, easy to digest or gluten-free. The following flours are great substitutes for your regular plain or wholemeal flours. Each behaves slightly differently, so following the recipes and experimenting with quantities when cooking will help you get to know which flours you enjoy working with and eating.

BESAN FLOUR is made from chickpeas and has a wonderful nutty flavour. It's a great gluten-free option for cakes, breads, pastry and savoury crêpes. The besan tarts on page 78 are always a big hit.

BROWN RICE FLOUR is a gluten-free flour that works best when combined with other flours in baked goods, such as my banana and coconut bread on page 82.

BUCKWHEAT FLOUR is a gluten-free flour that works well in both sweet and savoury baking, and for pancakes and crêpes.

COCONUT FLOUR is a flour made from dried coconut flesh. It's high in fibre, contains healthy fats and makes a great gluten- and nut-free alternative for baking and thickening foods. It absorbs liquid rapidly though, so will require more wet ingredients than your average flour. Look online for some guidance on the ratio of wet to dry ingredients before starting.

CORNFLOUR (CORNSTARCH) is finely ground flour made from corn. It works well for thickening sauces and stocks. I use brown rice and teff flour in a similar way.

QUINOA FLOUR is an unrefined flour made from quinoa. It's gluten-free and great for baking but can be strong in flavour, so it's best used with other ingredients that have robust flavours. See my pumpkin, carrot and herb loaf on page 168.

SPELT FLOUR is an ancient grain that, despite containing gluten, is much less refined than white flour and often easier for the digestive system to break down. It is a perfect substitute for anything where a wheat-based ingredient is used (you can substitute it in the same ratio).

BICARBONATE OF SODA (BAKING SODA) is a raising agent best used in baking when an acid (such as lemon juice, honey or chocolate) is present to create the rising reaction. It is also great mixed with water for chemical-free bench-top cleaning.

BAKING POWDER (I opt for aluminium- and gluten-free versions). This is a mix of sodium bicarbonate and cream of tartar which acts as a raising agent in baked goods.

RECIPE KEY The letters below are signposts to help you on your health journey. They indicate recipes (though not necessarily the serving suggestions) that fall under the categories below. Please note that this book uses the term 'sugar-free' to highlight dishes free from refined/white sugars.

GF · GLUTEN-FREE
DF · DAIRY-FREE
SF · SUGAR-FREE
V · VEGETARIAN
VG · VEGAN

GRAINS

Gluten-free grains are always in stock in my pantry. I like to mix them together to create a combination of different textures and flavours.

AMARANTH is a small gluten-free grain rich in calcium, iron and phosphorus. Cook it with other grains such as quinoa and brown rice.

BROWN, RED, BASMATI AND WILD RICE are some of my favourite go-to grains because they are filling, nutritious and incredibly versatile. See the red quinoa vegetarian sushi recipe on page 188.

BUCKWHEAT (hulled or unhulled) isn't technically a grain but rather a fruit seed from the rhubarb family. It is considered a 'pseudo-grain' and has a beautiful nutrition profile. Buckwheat works incredibly well after being soaked for recipes such as the bread on page 97, in dehydrated or sprouted form, or just cooked as you would rice to accompany hearty fare or toss through salads.

QUINOA is another fruit seed widely considered a pseudo-grain; it contains all the amino acids to make a complete protein, which is unusual for plant food. Quinoa cooks quickly and works in savoury and sweet dishes, such as the grilled stone fruit and pomegranate quinoa on page 92.

ROLLED SPELT works beautifully in place of traditional oats in breakfast foods, and is also great in stir-fries once soaked and drained with savoury accompaniments. Contains gluten.

STEEL-CUT AND ROLLED OATS make for wonderful breakfast options. They contain gluten, but are relatively easy on our digestive system and are rich in fibre.

LEGUMES AND PULSES

Keep a selection of pulses on hand in the pantry to add to salads, frittatas, curries, and to make dips and more. Lentils, butter beans, kidney beans and chickpeas are always in my pantry. Try the beetroot hummus on page 76 for your hit of legumes.

HERBS AND SPICES

I can't live without my overflowing (and completely chaotic) spice box. Herbs and spices bring new taste experiences and a host of nutritional benefits to a meal. To spice up even the simplest of meals try ...

BAY LEAVES, CAYENNE, CHILLI (FLAKED OR GROUND), CINNAMON (GROUND OR QUILLS), CORIANDER, CUMIN, GINGER, NUTMEG, OREGANO, PARSLEY, PAPRIKA (SMOKED AND SWEET) AND GROUND TURMERIC.

NATURAL SWEETENERS

Natural sweeteners are more widely available than ever before. If you haven't tried using them, I encourage you to give them a go in baking and treats. Bet you won't miss your old refined sugar.

COCONUT SUGAR resembles granulated sugar and is absolutely sensational for baking.

MAPLE SYRUP is sap from the maple tree. Look for 'pure' maple syrup when buying as there are lots of imitation syrups that are essentially sugar-flavoured with some caramel and maple-like flavours. Maple is a great vegan substitute for honey. I always opt for Canadian maple syrup.

MEDJOOL DATES are a great substitute for honey or maple syrup in baking. They are also great binders for raw treats.

RAW HONEY contains enzymes, antioxidants, vitamins and minerals that are great for immunity and longevity. Try not to 'cook' the honey at high heats as this destroys the nutrients.

RICE MALT SYRUP is created by converting brown rice starches into sugars. Rice malt syrup does not contain fructose.

VANILLA is so special in all sorts of desserts and sweet treats. I keep vanilla beans, paste, powder and extract in the kitchen and use them all in different ways.

NUTS AND SEEDS

These are a great source of protein, minerals and healthy fats. I keep big jars of nuts and seeds in my kitchen for sprinkling over salads, breakfasts, snacks — you name it!

ALMONDS, BRAZIL NUTS, CASHEWS, LINSEEDS, PECANS PEPITAS (PUMPKIN SEEDS), SESAME SEEDS, SUNFLOWER SEEDS AND WALNUTS.

CHIA SEEDS are small black or white seeds with a complete amino acid profile. They are rich in fibre and fats and a great vegan substitute for eggs in baking or fritters. Combine 1 tbsp of chia seeds with 3 tbsp of water and allow to soak to create a chia gel.

NUT AND SEED SPREADS are so useful in the kitchen to top with both sweet and savoury items on toast or crackers, pop in smoothies, porridge and baked goods, and to bind and create delicious caramels in raw treats.

OILS

There are so many beautiful oils and they all do slightly different jobs; some are great for cooking, some are better for salad dressings. Having a small range of oils in your kitchen will bring a lot of different flavours and health benefits to your cooking.

ALMOND OIL is rich in vitamin E and monounsaturated fatty acids. It's best used as a raw oil.

COCONUT OIL comes from coconut flesh and is cold-pressed to create an oil rich with anti-fungal, anti-bacterial and anti-viral properties. It is solid when cold and liquid when warmed. When a recipe calls for melted coconut oil, ensure it is fully melted as this changes the structure of the final product.

EXTRA VIRGIN OLIVE OIL is best used raw on salads and steamed vegetables. Only cook over very low heat as the properties of the oil are unstable when exposed to heat and light.

GRAPESEED OIL is pressed from the seeds of grapes. It is versatile in cooking as it has a neutral flavour.

SESAME OIL is delicious in Asian dressings and quite rich in flavour so you don't need to use much to experience it in a dish.

TRUFFLE OIL is an olive oil infused with black or white truffles. Truffles have a unique flavour and are a deeply aromatic funghi. A real treat.

WALNUT OIL is great brain food and best used as a raw oil for salads and steamed vegetables.

PLANT-BASED MILKS

Where once only dairy and soy milk existed, there are now so many alternatives available, which is great news for anyone suffering from lactose intolerance.

Almond, walnut, cashew and coconut milks are permanent residents in my pantry and fridge. Don't hold back from making your own; walnut, almond and cashew milk are all very easy to make at home using simple tools.

To make your own milks, the general ratio is $\frac{1}{4}$ cup of nuts to 1 litre (35 fl oz/4 cups) of water, blitzed in a high-speed blender until smooth and then strained through a nut-milk bag. Store in a glass jar in the fridge for 1 week.

SEASONINGS

A few more staples that add lots of flavour with little effort.

NUTRITIONAL YEAST is an inactive yeast rich in B vitamins for energy. It has a cheesy flavour that makes it a great vegan substitute for cheese in recipes. I often use it in risottos such as the one on page 214.

PEPPER — either whole black peppercorns or freshly ground black pepper — is a must.

SALT is crucial in just about every dish. I like having a few types on hand. Sea, Celtic and Himalayan salts all have a much better flavour and mineral content than standard iodised table salt.

TAMARI is a gluten-free alternative to soy sauce.

SUPERFOODS

These small but mighty ingredients pack a major nutritional punch, and a little of them goes a long way.

ACAI are small red berries from the rainforests of South America. They play a powerful role as antioxidants within the body. Great in smoothies.

BEE POLLEN, small granules of pollen harvested from beehives, is quite sweet in flavour. It is rich in protein, with a good supply of free amino acids that can be readily used by our bodies. It is beautiful sprinkled into smoothies (see the summer berry breakfast smoothie on page 90).

CACAO is a mineral-dense and antioxidant-rich powder. Not only is it insanely delicious, it's also a great source of magnesium for muscle relaxation and energy, and can stabilise and improve your mood. Made from the cacao pod, raw cacao has a rich chocolate flavour and is a nutritional powerhouse. It tastes amazing both raw and cooked. Try it in my self-saucing chocolate pudding on page 180. Carob powder tastes great as a substitute for cacao, if you prefer it.

CAMU, a small citrus fruit from South America, is another incredibly antioxidant-rich ingredient. Wonderful in both sweet and savoury dishes.

MACA is a powder that comes from the maca root. It has a lovely caramel flavour and is great for endocrine support.

PSYLLIUM HUSK is a great source of soluble fibre, acting as a wonderful binder in the likes of breads. See my buckwheat seed bread on page 97.

SLIPPERY ELM is derived from the inner bark of the slippery elm tree, and when mixed into food and drinks it thickens and becomes slightly gel-like. This gel coats and soothes the mouth, throat and intestines. I use it in the almond milk hot chocolate on page 232.

SPIRULINA is a dark green algae with a rich supply of minerals, particularly iron, making it a great addition to the diet for vegetarians and vegans. Pop it in raw treats, smoothies and pesto, such as my kale and almond version on page 28.

WAKAME, DULSE AND NORI seaweeds are packed with minerals and are a great source of iron. They add a beautiful marine saltiness to salads such as the warm mushroom and pine nut salad on page 192.

TEAS

A selection of herbal teas are a must for cuppas with friends or to brew ahead of time and chill for serving in big jugs at special occasions. Dandelion, peppermint, chamomile, green, rooibos (red bush) and licorice teas are always in my pantry.

VINEGARS

Like oils, there are many wonderful vinegars available and it's a good idea to have a couple on hand in your kitchen. They keep for ages and each has their own particular personality and use. Try experimenting with a few types to find out which ones you prefer. These are two of my favourites.

APPLE CIDER VINEGAR is the fermented carbohydrate of apples. It is slightly fruity in taste and a great health tonic. Look for an apple cider vinegar sold with 'the mother', which is an amino-acid based substance that acts as a 'starter'. This indicates that the product is a good-quality vinegar. Use in dressings and marinades.

BALSAMIC VINEGAR is much sweeter than apple cider vinegar. Its flavour is perfect for using in reductions, dressings and also for marinades.

in the fridge

Fruit and vegetables vary by season but the usual suspects in my fridge are kale, spinach, rocket (arugula), tomatoes, zucchini (courgette), beetroot (beets), carrots, capsicum (pepper), cucumber, pumpkin, leek, lemons, limes and seasonal fruits.

DAIRY

I don't consume a large amount of dairy, but there are definitely a few staples I can't live without.

BUTTER I like to use hand-cultured or organic.

CHEESES such as goat's cheese, ricotta, parmesan and pecorino make regular appearances in my recipes.

EGGS are always on hand in my fridge. I use them a lot for quick meal solutions. It's worth spending a little more on organic or free-range eggs if you can, as eggs from happy hens give optimal nutritional benefits.

MILK — preferably organic dairy milk (if tolerated; if not, there are wonderful natural plant alternatives available).

YOGHURT is so versatile. If I'm using dairy yoghurt, then organic natural or Greek-style yoghurts are my favourites. Otherwise, I love coconut yoghurt, which is a wonderful dairy-free alternative. For me, full-fat dairy products are the only way to go because low-fat dairy is often higher in sugar, added to compensate for the taste lost when the fat is taken out.

Those products also lack the nutritional benefits of whole milk.

HERBS

Which fresh herbs you have in your fridge is a matter of personal preference, but my fridge is always stocked with coriander (cilantro), flat-leaf (Italian) parsley, dill and mint. They keep well and add so much flavour and minerals to meals.

Just as essential for adding fresh flavour and a host of nutritional benefits are ingredients like ginger, garlic and fresh turmeric, which are also on heavy rotation in my house.

FERMENTED FOODS

These types of food are the golden key to good gut health. Just a spoonful or glass a day of these can work wonders.

KOMBUCHA is made from a symbiotic culture of bacteria and yeast. Ginger and lemon or green tea-infused kombucha are my favourite evening aperitif drink. Great for detox dinners.

SAUERKRAUT AND KIMCHI are great to add to meals or munch on between meals to support digestion and immunity.

IN THE FREEZER

We all have days that get away from us. Stock your freezer so you always have a nutritious solution to hand at a moment's notice.

BREADS — especially home-baked — are great in the freezer. I usually freeze a savoury option such as my buckwheat seed bread (page 97), as well as my banana and coconut bread (page 82). Perfect for meals or quick snacks.

FRUITS like blueberries, strawberries, raspberries, mango cheeks, bananas and coconut flesh are great to freeze then use in smoothies or quick desserts.

LEFTOVERS are lifesavers! Having a little stash of leftovers for easy meals is always a good thing. Soups and stews in particular freeze really well.

SNACKS like raw treats will last a couple of extra weeks if they are frozen (according to storage instructions). I'll usually keep a few different flavours of raw balls and some kind of slice or some raw chocolate in there for an unexpected guest.

VEGETABLES — peas, broccoli and spinach are always in my freezer.

tools for the kitchen

I've built up my kitchen gadgets over time, and I encourage anyone who is a keen foodie or entertainer to do the same. Having a few good tools really does make food prep that much easier. There are a few items on the page opposite that I absolutely love, but if someone said I could only take one of them with me to a desert island, it would definitely be my set of sharp knives!

APPLIANCES

There are only two major appliances I think you need in a kitchen these days: a food processor and high-speed blender. They serve multiple purposes and everything else is best done with your own two hands. It's valuable to learn the art of whisking, folding, kneading and combining ingredients — I believe this truly enhances your understanding of food, texture, nutrition and flavour.

BAKEWARE

A 20 cm (8 inch) square glass or ceramic baking dish; large oval or rectangular 20 × 30 cm (8 × 12 inch) ceramic baking dish; loaf (bar) tin; 12-hole standard muffin tin; 20 cm (8 inch) round spring-form cake tin; small 12-hole silicon cupcake mould; and two rectangular baking trays that fit your oven perfectly should cover most baking eventualities.

GLASS JARS

Admittedly I have an obsession with glass jars, so to not include these would be like walking around in one shoe. They are an integral part of the way my kitchen operates and, honestly, once you start organising your shelves with them, life, cooking and catering becomes so much clearer. Glass jars are also great for storing fresh juices, smoothies, marinades, dressings, dips, nut milks, etc. in the fridge. You don't need to go out and buy a whole heap of them either; invest in airtight, snap-sealed jars for larger quantities of dry ingredients such as flours, grains and flaked coconut. Buy nuts and seeds in bulk and then keep smaller jars from your food purchases to store these as well as superfood powders, crackers, spices, teas and other small ingredients.

KNIVES

The best thing you can do is watch a chef demonstrate the art of sharpening, and then invest in a simple steel to keep your knives at their best. It may seem counterintuitive, but you are more likely to have an accident in the kitchen if your knives are blunt. Sharp knives are the key to easy food preparation and beautifully presented meals. At the bare minimum, aim to have a carving, chef's and paring knife. As your foodie passions progress, so will your collection of (and appreciation for) well-made high-quality knives.

MANDOLIN

Don't underestimate the power of this tiny tool! I could not live without mine for so many reasons, but primarily because it (quickly) creates the most beautiful finely shaved vegetables to toss through salads.

PLASTIC TRAYS

These sound a strange tool to include in this list, I know, but about six basic plastic trays (easily found in supermarkets) will help you immensely with food preparation and storage in the fridge. If you are making canapés for a cocktail party or even just slicing your vegetables so they are ready to throw together at the last minute before cooking, trays will help to make this easy.

POTS, PANS AND THE LIKE

Small and large frying pans that can go from stovetop to oven; small and medium saucepans (with strainers); a large stockpot; and a French oven (large flameproof casserole dish) for slow-cooking meats, stews or curries — these will see you through the best of cooking moments. A deep roasting tray with a rack that fits your oven perfectly is also a must.

STORAGE CONTAINERS

A couple of larger storage containers are great for bigger occasions when you need to marinate meat or fish, or store extra batches of things, like tarts or an abundance of fresh herbs.

creating moments

Memories really come from experience or the moments shared at an occasion. And while nothing beats laughter, smiles and warmth, there are a few little things that can help build these moments into something really special. Simple things like ...

FLOWERS

These are, of course, seasonal, but whatever the season floral arrangements bring life to a table, either in larger arrangements or dotted around the room in small vases, milk bottles or jars. The scent of flowers is always something you notice in a room as you enter it, so choosing flowers that have beautiful scents is all part of creating an experience for your guests.

FRUIT AND VEGETABLES

I love pulling elements of the recipes I'm serving into the decorating of the table. They create a talking point or memory for your guests. Instead of vases of flowers, try filling small jars with fresh herbs or fill bigger vases with leaves such as kale and spinach. Arrange vines of baby truss tomatoes among the dishes so your guests can enjoy their colour and maybe even graze on them before the meal if they wish. Simple things like weighing down a name card

with a pear or apple, or a variety of fruits, a different one for each guest, is a fun way to weave seasonal nutrition, colour and style into your event.

GLASS VASES AND JARS

Much like my obsession with using glass jars for storage, I adore using glassware for entertaining. Just in case you had any doubt, glass vases and jars are some of the most versatile pieces I own for entertaining. If I'm presenting crackers on a cheeseboard, I like arranging the crackers so they spill out of a jar on its side; I also like to fill old maple syrup jars with small blooms and place those around a table. Upturned jam jars can act as tealight candle-holders on a platter or around a room, and sometimes I'll flip a large vase upside down to create a higher tier in my table arrangement. Let me tell you, glass is where it's at!

KNICK KNACKS

I am forever dashing into vintage homeware stores, op shops or random home shops in the hope of uncovering something special for the next occasion. And trust me, I do! Some of my best finds have been by chance, so keep your eyes peeled. It might be a simple jug, random sets of cups and saucers in different colours or designs, retro glass plates or baskets, napkins, linens, tea towels, tin or wooden boxes ... you just never know when or where the perfect item will wander into your life, but they can be some of the greatest presentation treasures in entertaining.

MATCHING COLOURS TO THE SEASONS:

Spring always feels right with greens, light greys and neutrals to freshen things up. *Summer* is a great chance to use vibrant bold colours such as blues and yellows contrasted with crisp white touches.

CONSIDER THE COLOURS OF THE SEASON AND KEEP AN EYE OUT FOR ANYTHING THAT LENDS ITSELF NATURALLY TO THE THEME

Autumn is a time for rustic, earthy oranges, reds and ochres complemented with neutrals. *Winter* months suit navy, cream, rich browns, darker greys or charcoal.

MATERIALS AND RIBBONS

I tend to collect cuts of random materials and ribbons here and there because I love using them to add colour and vibrance to the entertaining experience. Longer strips of material can be great for using as tablemats or runners, while smaller offcuts can be used on platters, tied around vases, jars or chairs, or used with napkins and name cards. Because I create occasions throughout the year, I consider the colours of the season and keep an eye out for anything that lends itself naturally to the theme I'm planning.

NATURAL ELEMENTS

If I have a larger table abundant with bright vegetables or even foods that aren't as bright and in need a pop of colour, I'll often use a big banana leaf or something similar to give the table a real lift and sense of life. I pick up fronds that have fallen from trees, give them a good clean out, then line them with material and present breads or other snacks in them. If you walk through your neighbourhood you'll find these types of natural materials for your occasion fairly easily. They are lovely to admire in a room, or on a platter or table, and complement all foods beautifully.

PRESENTATION PLATTERS

These can take a little longer to discover but they are very worthwhile to have. Again, my tip is to start simply with just three types of white ceramic platters: a round, a square and a long rectangle. Many supermarkets these days stock different sizes of serving platters, which are great for entertaining small groups in style. I also love presenting food on big antique chopping boards or pieces of marble.

TABLEWARE

If you don't already have serveware that you love, keep your eyes peeled for items that will be versatile enough to suit any occasion. My tip is to start with a simple white crockery setting and a full set of cutlery. These items make such a big difference to setting a table and don't have to be expensive. Once you have these basics, start to collect special little pieces here and there to complement them. If there are local designers near you making beautiful ceramics, support them by treating yourself to one or two unique pieces you love. It is these special little touches that can elevate occasions like a high tea, long lunch or a casual dinner to something personal and memorable.

spring

I am not alone in celebrating the arrival of spring; fresh scents in the air, brighter mornings and the yearning our bodies seem to have to simply refresh. Each year, at the start of spring, I like to embark on a little lifestyle spring clean. Out goes the dust accumulating in the different areas of my life and in comes the new. When it comes to diet, a spring clean looks light, fresh, delicate and green: green because there is a beautiful abundance of seasonal, green vegetables around, which provide us with exactly what our bodies need at this time of year. These are the foods that will help cleanse and renew.

Entertaining in spring is so delightful because the food is fresh and the weather makes entertaining outside an option again. You have a chance to inspire the health of those around you by creating lighter dishes, full of beautiful ingredients. When I think of spring entertaining I think of cleansing meals, picnics, high teas and light lunches in the sunshine with friends. Then, before you know it, you're rolling into the summer feeling lighter, happier and more nourished than ever.

SPRING FRUITS

APPLE
AVOCADO
BANANA
BLOOD ORANGE
BLUEBERRIES
CHERRIES
GRAPEFRUIT
LEMON
LOQUAT
MANDARIN
MANGO
MELON
MULBERRIES
PAPAYA
PASSIONFRUIT
PAW PAW
PINEAPPLE
POMELO
ROCK MELON
STRAWBERRIES
TANGELO
VALENCIA
 ORANGE

SPRING VEGETABLES

ARTICHOKE
ASPARAGUS
BEETROOT
 (BEETS)
BROAD BEANS
BROCCOLI
CABBAGE
CARROT
CAULIFLOWER
CHILLI
CUCUMBER
GARLIC
GREEN BEANS
KALE
LETTUCE
MUSHROOM
PEAS
POTATO
SILVERBEET
SPINACH
SWEETCORN
TOMATO
WATERCRESS
ZUCCHINI
 (COURGETTE)
 & ZUCCHINI
 FLOWERS

the cleansing lunch

The first time I invited friends to a cleansing lunch, the invitation received a somewhat mixed response. And with a reaction like that, I knew it was my job to ensure that anyone who doubted, even momentarily, the beauty of a detox lunch as I had pitched it had to be completely convinced with the very first mouthful. Thankfully, they were!

People have different ideas of what a detox or a cleanse should be and which processes and nutritional elements are involved. My approach is to keep the focus on clean, light foods that are easy on the digestive system. I also include a good dose of bitter and sour flavours to aid digestion and help the body absorb and use the available nutrients. Supplement a clean detox meal with hydration from lovely herbal teas (hot or chilled), filtered water with a squeeze of lemon or lime and try serving small shots of herb-spiked smoothies or chilled green soups before lunch, to up the nutrients and set the tone for a lean, clean afternoon together.

SERVES 4

MAINS

STEAMED WHITE FISH WITH LEMON GINGER VINAIGRETTE

POACHED CHICKEN BREAST WITH KALE AND ALMOND PESTO DRESSING

SIDES

TURMERIC, QUINOA AND CORN SALAD

CAULIFLOWER 'RICE' AND SILVERBEET SALAD

QUEEN OF DETOX SALAD

DRINKS

CORI-PINEAPPLE MINT SMASH

LEMONGRASS TEA

TURMERIC, QUINOA AND CORN SALAD [ABOVE LEFT] *recipe page 30;* POACHED CHICKEN
BREAST WITH KALE AND ALMOND PESTO DRESSING [ABOVE RIGHT] *recipe page 28*

Steaming foods is one of the most nutritious methods of cooking because the food retains so many of its nutrients. On top of that, it is fast, easy and results in mild flavours that pair really well with stronger ones, such as the ginger and chilli used here.

Steamed white fish with lemon ginger vinaigrette

GF / DF / SF

4 x 125 g (4½ oz) white fish fillets (barramundi, snapper, ling or dory), scaled and pinboned
1 spring onion (scallion), white part only, finely sliced into long strips, to garnish

Lemon ginger vinaigrette
2 teaspoons freshly grated ginger
2 tablespoons extra virgin olive oil
1 teaspoon apple cider vinegar
1 tablespoon lemon juice
a pinch of finely grated lemon zest
½ teaspoon finely chopped red chilli or dried chilli flakes

Bring a large saucepan of water to the boil and check that a large steamer basket can sit comfortably over the pan without touching the water.

Wrap the fish in baking paper, place in the steamer basket over the boiling water and cover. Steam for 10–12 minutes, or until cooked through. While the fish is steaming, combine the vinaigrette ingredients in a small bowl.

Remove the fish from the steamer and unwrap it, then arrange on a platter. Drizzle over the vinaigrette and garnish with the spring onion.

SERVES 4

Poaching ingredients is another really easy and nutritious way of cooking. It keeps meals clean and light, and maintains the highest levels of nutrients (and moisture) of all the cooking methods. Like steaming, poaching also creates mild flavours that pair beautifully with vibrant flavours, such as this pesto. I toss this versatile pesto through courgette pasta, mash it into boiled eggs, turn it into a dressing, mix it with mayo to create a pesto crème, or spread it through a lasagne instead of a cream sauce.

Poached chicken breast with kale and almond pesto dressing

GF / DF / SF   KALE AND ALMOND PESTO GF / DF / SF / V / VG

400 g (14 oz) skinless,
    boneless chicken breasts
4 tablespoons kale and
    almond pesto (see below)
2 tablespoons cold-pressed
    extra virgin olive oil
1 tablespoon lemon juice

Kale and almond pesto
125 g (4½ oz) kale leaves
    (weight includes stalks)
1 large garlic clove,
    finely sliced
40 g (1½ oz/½ a bunch)
    coriander (cilantro),
    stems and leaves (or any
    herbs of your choice)
85 g (3 oz/½ cup) almonds
    (skins on)
185 ml (6 fl oz/¾ cup)
    cold-pressed extra virgin
    olive oil
½ teaspoon nutritional
    yeast
¼ teaspoon spirulina
juice of ½ a lemon or lime
sea salt and freshly ground
    black pepper, to taste

Fill a medium-sized saucepan with water and bring to the boil. Add the chicken breasts, bring back to the boil once again then turn off the heat and cover with a lid. Poach the chicken for 30 minutes, then drain.

While the chicken is poaching, make the pesto. Strip and discard the stalks from the kale leaves then wash the leaves well. Place all of the pesto ingredients in a food processor and blend until you have a beautiful textured pesto. Taste and season again, if needed.

In a small bowl, whisk together 4 tablespoons of the pesto with the olive oil and lemon juice to create a pesto dressing.

Slice the drained chicken evenly into 1 cm (½ inch) thick slices so it retains all that gorgeous moisture from the poaching. Arrange on a serving platter then drizzle over the pesto dressing and serve immediately.

NOTE

You can more or less choose your own adventure with the herbs or greens in the pesto here — just ensure you use good-quality extra virgin olive oil and almonds to make the flavours shine.

SERVES 4
PESTO MAKES 200 ML (7 FL OZ)

Turmeric is my golden spice when it comes to nutrition; it is used in Ayurveda, a traditional Indian form of medicine based on achieving balance between the body's systems using diet, herbs and meditative breathing. It contains powerful nutrients such as curcumin, which can help reduce inflammation in the body, making it a wonderful addition to other detox nutrients in a cleansing meal. This salad is delicious as is, but wonderful with a piece of grilled fish or chicken for an evening meal, too.

Turmeric, quinoa and corn salad

GF / DF / SF / V / VG

100 g (3½ oz/½ cup) quinoa
1 teaspoon ground turmeric
1 teaspoon ground
  fenugreek
1 teaspoon yellow
  mustard seeds
75 g (2¾ oz/½ cup) currants
40 g (1½ oz/½ a bunch)
  coriander (cilantro),
  leaves picked and stalks
  finely chopped
2 sweetcorn cobs, kernels
  sliced off the husk
3 kale leaves, stems
  discarded, leaves washed
  and roughly torn
35 g (1¼ oz/¼ cup) slivered
  almonds, lightly toasted

Lemony coconut dressing
1 tablespoon lemon juice
4 tablespoons coconut
  cream or coconut milk
1 tablespoon olive oil
a pinch of cayenne or
  chilli powder
sea salt and freshly ground
  black pepper, to taste

Put the quinoa in a large saucepan with 375 ml (13 fl oz/1½ cups) of boiling water, the turmeric, fenugreek, mustard seeds and currants. Cover with a lid and bring to the boil. Once boiling, remove the lid, reduce the heat and simmer for around 10 minutes, or until all of the liquid has been absorbed. Make sure the quinoa is soft and cooked before removing from the heat. If not, add another 125 ml (4 fl oz/½ cup) of boiling water and continue to cook for a few minutes more.

Once cooked, spoon the quinoa into a large serving bowl. Add the coriander stalks and corn, and toss to combine, then leave for a few minutes to cool slightly.

Meanwhile, put all of the dressing ingredients in a bowl and mix together with a fork.

Toss the coriander leaves and kale through the quinoa mixture and stir in half the almonds. Drizzle the dressing over the top of the salad and top with remaining almonds.

SERVES 4

Cauliflower comes from the cruciferous or brassica family, which includes vegetables such as broccoli, cabbage, brussels sprouts and watercress. It contains a powerful sulphur compound, sulforaphane, which some believe can help to slow tumour growth in certain cancers, improve blood pressure and kidney function, and support liver detoxification. For these reasons (and because it is delicious), cauliflower is especially good for anyone who wants to boost their nutrition and cleanse their system.

Cauliflower 'rice' and silverbeet salad

GF / DF / SF / V / VG

375 g (13 oz/3 cups)
   cauliflower florets
4 silverbeet (Swiss chard)
   leaves, finely sliced,
   stalks included
a handful of mint leaves,
   finely sliced
seeds from 1 pomegranate
2 tablespoons dried
   cranberries (currants,
   sour cherries or raisins
   also work well)
2 spring onions (scallions),
   whites and greens
   finely sliced
2 tablespoons pine nuts,
   lightly toasted

Cumin dressing
2 tablespoons extra virgin
   olive oil
2 tablespoons lemon juice
1 teaspoon ground cumin
sea salt and freshly ground
   black pepper, to taste

'Rice' your raw cauliflower by pulsing it in a food processor for a couple of seconds, until it resembles a crumb or rice-like texture. Combine in a serving bowl with the remaining salad ingredients and toss to combine.

Combine the dressing ingredients in a small bowl, then drizzle over the salad, toss to dress, and serve.

SERVES 4

Sour and bitter flavours stimulate the liver and improve detoxification, so I've combined a range of sour and bitter vegetables and fruits for this salad to really give the liver a nudge. Beetroot is great for a liver detox as it contains betaine, which stimulates liver cells to move toxins out of the body while protecting the liver and bile ducts. As well as being great for you, this salad is fairly robust, so it keeps well if you want to make up a batch for easy weekday lunches. Add a piece of grilled chicken and you also have a quick dinner.

Queen of Detox salad

GF / DF / SF / VG/ V

35 g (1¼ oz/1 cup firmly packed) rocket (arugula) leaves

75 g (2¾ oz/1 cup) shredded red cabbage, lightly packed (approximately ⅛ of a small red cabbage)

1 witlof (endive) heart, leaves separated

1 radicchio, leaves separated

5 or 6 small baby radishes, finely sliced

100 g (3½ oz) beetroot (beets), peeled and finely sliced or shaved

40 g (1½ oz/¼ cup) red onion, finely sliced then soaked in cold water for 30 minutes, if time allows, then drained

1 small ruby grapefruit, skin and pith sliced off and discarded, segmented

1 blood or regular orange, skin and pith sliced off and discarded, segmented

55 g (2 oz/⅓ cup) pepitas (pumpkin seeds)

40 g (1½ oz/⅓ cup) walnut halves

40 g (1½ oz/¼ cup) sunflower seeds

salt and freshly ground black pepper, to taste

Dressing

2 tablespoons extra virgin olive oil

2 tablespoons lemon juice

1 teaspoon ground cinnamon

1 teaspoon ground cumin

1 small garlic clove, crushed

a pinch of finely chopped fresh chilli or dried chilli flakes (optional)

Combine all the salad ingredients in a large serving bowl and toss together lightly.

Mix the dressing ingredients in a small jar, shake well and then drizzle over the salad, tossing lightly once again so all ingredients have a gentle glisten.

SERVES 4

Cori-pineapple mint smash

GF / DF / SF / V / VG

Pineapple is rich in the digestive enzyme bromelain. Consuming a small amount of this blended smash before or between meals can boost your digestive enzymes, preparing your gastrointestinal system to break down your next meal and better absorb the nutrients from it. I suggest serving this in shot glasses or in short glasses, to welcome your guests.

320 g (11¼ oz/2 cups) roughly chopped pineapple
175 g (6 oz/1 cup) roughly chopped
  Lebanese cucumber
a handful of mint leaves
a handful of coriander (cilantro) leaves
500 ml (17 fl oz/2 cups) coconut water

Place all of the ingredients in a high-powered blender and blitz until smooth. Serve chilled or at room temperature in shot glasses.

SERVES 4–6

Lemongrass tea

GF / DF / SF / V / VG

A tea like this one is a refreshing, cleansing end to a meal. Lemongrass acts as a diuretic, supporting the kidney's detoxification and elimination process. If you want to dress this tea up for the table, slices of lemon, orange or lime make nice flavour combinations; fresh mint or basil leaves with some sliced ginger is also lovely.

2 lemongrass stalks
1 litre (35 fl oz/4 cups) boiling water

Trim the bottom ends of the lemongrass and then halve each stalk lengthways. Bruise the stalks: one at a time, lay the blade of a large knife flat over the lemongrass, then use the heel of your hand to strike the widest part of the knife so it flattens the stalks. This helps to release the flavours.

Place the stalks in a large ceramic jug and add the boiling water. Cover and allow to infuse for 10 minutes, then serve.

SERVES 4

LEMONGRASS TEA

a healthier high tea

High tea conjures up all sorts of images of fluffy white sandwiches and heavy sweets — not such healthy images for many of us. That's why I love to make my high tea a little differently: in a way that makes you feel good the moment you lay your eyes on it. High tea is about being able to sit down and enjoy the whole experience together, so no one should need to go to the kitchen during the meal (unless, of course, it's to boil another pot of tea). When creating a menu for high tea, I try to balance the sweet with the savoury items and include certain foods that are nostalgic and warm people's hearts.

You don't need to have tiered cake stands, fine china or silver to create a beautiful high-tea setting; be creative with what is around you. Choose a theme for the occasion and build different components of that theme into the setting. Create tiers by using platters and small plates balanced on upturned jars or vases, use ribbons pinned across the tablecloth to pick out the different colours in the food, drop a few delicate flower petals around the platters to bring everything together, and don't be afraid to be a little mismatched with your teapots of nourishing herbal teas.

SERVES 12

SAVOURY

SMOKED TROUT ON BUCKWHEAT BLINIS

ZUCCHINI AND GOAT'S CHEESE ON SEED SNAPS WITH A CRISPY OLIVE CRUMB

LAMB FILLET WITH BEETROOT HUMMUS AND ROCKET

CHICKEN SANDWICHES

SWEET

PECAN CRUNCH COOKIES

RAW CARROT CAKES

PASSIONFRUIT SHORTBREADS

RAW ALMOND CARAMEL SLICE

DRINKS

ICED DANDELION TEA

WHITE PEACH AND BANANA SMOOTHIE

SMOKED TROUT ON
BUCKWHEAT BLINIS
recipe page 42

ZUCCHINI AND GOAT'S
CHEESE ON SEED
SNAPS WITH A CRISPY
OLIVE CRUMB
recipe page 43

PASSIONFRUIT SHORTBREADS
recipe page 50

WHITE PEACH AND BANANA
SMOOTHIE *recipe page 51*

Blinis have been gracing platters at cocktail parties, high teas and special events for as long as I can remember. For good reason: they're always a hit! I've remade this old-time favourite using buckwheat flour instead of wheat flour, and avocado in place of crème fraîche. The colours and flavours combine beautifully to celebrate the blini. An oldie, but a goodie.

Smoked trout on buckwheat blinis

GF / DF / SF

Buckwheat blinis

1 egg
125 ml (4 fl oz/½ cup) milk
80 g (2¾ oz/⅔ cup)
   buckwheat flour
½ teaspoon aluminium- and
   gluten-free baking powder
¼ teaspoon bicarbonate of
   soda (baking soda)
coconut or grapeseed oil,
   for cooking

Topping

½ an avocado, flesh diced
   into 5 mm (¼ inch) pieces
1 teaspoon finely grated
   horseradish, either fresh
   or from a jar
1 tablespoon lemon juice
120 g (4¼ oz) hot-smoked
   trout, flaked into
   small pieces
a small handful of dill
freshly ground black pepper

To make the blinis, combine the egg and milk in a jug and whisk well. Sift the buckwheat flour, baking powder and bicarbonate of soda into a medium bowl, mix to combine, then make a well in the centre. Pour the milk mixture into the well, whisking as you go until combined, then set aside for approximately 10 minutes.

Place a large frying pan over a medium heat and add a drop of coconut or grapeseed oil, spreading the oil around the pan. Drop 2 teaspoons of batter per blini into the pan and cook for 2 minutes on each side, or until lightly golden. Approximately 6 blinis should fit in the pan at a time. Move them to a

plate lined with paper towels as they cook and allow to cool.

To make the topping, lightly toss together the avocado, horseradish and lemon juice in a small bowl. Be careful not to over-toss or the avocado will lose its shape and become mushy.

Lay the blinis out on a serving tray or board and divide the avocado mixture evenly between them. Top with the smoked trout and dill, then finish with a good grind of pepper.

MAKES 12 CANAPÉS, 1 PER PERSON

Photograph page 40

Goat's cheese is quite a strongly flavoured creamy cheese that I use often: on canapés, as a spread on buckwheat bread, crumbled through salads ... Those who cannot tolerate cow's milk can often digest goat's cheese as it contains less lactose. If you don't want to fry the olives for the olive crumb, you can finely dice them. However, I really like the saltiness and crispiness of the olives when they are prepared in this way.

Zucchini and goat's cheese on seed snaps with a crispy olive crumb

GF / SF / V

12 bite-sized seed snaps (see recipe on page 70)

50 g (1¾ oz/⅓ cup) goat's cheese

¼ of a small red onion, very finely sliced and soaked in water for 30 minutes, if time allows, then drained

½ a small zucchini (courgette), finely shaved into ribbons

2 tablespoons ricotta cheese, quark, cottage cheese, or Greek-style yoghurt

¼ of a lemon

12 small flat-leaf (Italian) parsley leaves

Olive crumb

3 tablespoons grapeseed oil

45 g (1¾ oz/¼ cup) pitted and finely chopped Kalamata olives

To make the olive crumb, heat a small saucepan over a medium heat and add the grapeseed oil. After about 3 minutes, add the olives and cook on a medium–high heat for 6 minutes, or until the olives are lovely and crispy. Remove the olives from the saucepan and leave to drain on paper towels.

Arrange the seed snaps on a tray, spacing them evenly, then top each with a ¼ of a teaspoon of goat's cheese. Follow this with a slice of red onion and some zucchini. Top with ½ a teaspoon of ricotta, then squeeze a touch of lemon juice over each canapé. Sprinkle the olive crumb evenly on top, then garnish each canapé with a small parsley leaf and serve.

MAKES 12 CANAPÉS, 1 PER PERSON

Photograph page 40

Of all the canapés I make, this is probably one of my favourites because the colours are as much a treat for the eyes as the flavours are for the tastebuds. The lamb provides a real protein punch, and the bright hues of beetroot hummus alongside the green rocket and perfectly cooked lamb make an insanely pretty (and delicious) combination. Buy big rocket leaves for this, not the baby leaves that often come in bags, as you need the rocket to act as a sort of parcel for the hummus and lamb.

Lamb fillet with beetroot hummus and rocket

GF / DF / SF

200 g (7 oz) lamb fillet
  or backstrap, at room
  temperature
1 teaspoon balsamic
  vinegar
sea salt and freshly ground
  black pepper
1 teaspoon grapeseed oil
12 rocket (arugula) leaves
80 g (2¾ oz/⅓ cup) beetroot
  (beet) hummus
  (see page 76)
a small handful of snow
  pea (mangetout) sprouts

Place the lamb fillet on a board then drizzle over the balsamic vinegar, season generously with salt and pepper and rub the vinegar and seasoning all over the meat.

Heat the grapeseed oil on a high heat in a frying pan then add the lamb fillet. Cook for approximately 6 minutes, turning every couple of minutes to ensure the meat browns evenly. Remove from the pan, wrap in foil and allow to rest for about 15 minutes. Once cooled, slice into 24 thin pieces.

Trim the stalks of the rocket leaves then arrange them on a serving board. Place 1 teaspoon of beetroot hummus onto each rocket leaf, followed by a few pea sprouts and 2 slices of lamb. Season with salt and pepper, then serve.

MAKES 12 CANAPÉS, 1 PER PERSON

Chicken sandwiches are more or less a must for a high tea. The key to the chicken sandwich maintaining its lovely height is not to press down too firmly with your fingertips while slicing it. Cut softly or, even better, use an electric knife. When I plan a high tea event, I often ask my local baker to mix activated charcoal powder into the bread dough to create black sandwiches — this always creates a real stand-out experience and gets people talking. If you are on good terms with your local baker, or if you have a bread maker you use at home, this is a great option. About one tablespoon per loaf will give you gorgeous black bread.

Chicken sandwiches

DF / SF

500 g (1 lb 2 oz) skinless,
   boneless chicken breasts
500 g (1 lb 2 oz) skinless,
   boneless chicken thighs
70 g (2½ oz/½ cup) finely
   diced celery
185 g (6½ oz/¾ cup)
   good-quality mayonnaise
2 tablespoons finely
   chopped dill
3 tablespoons finely
   chopped basil leaves
2 tablespoons finely
   chopped flat-leaf (Italian)
   parsley leaves
2 spring onions (scallions),
   white parts only,
   finely chopped
1 teaspoon sea salt
freshly ground black
   pepper
1 loaf of spelt bread
   (or your bread of choice),
   thinly sliced for finger
   sandwiches
100 g (3½ oz) butter,
   softened

Bring a large saucepan of water to the boil. Place the chicken breasts and thighs in the water, bring back to the boil, then immediately turn off the heat, cover with a lid and leave to poach for 30 minutes. Drain and allow to cool.

Once cooled, dice the chicken into small pieces then put in a large bowl with the celery, mayonnaise, herbs, spring onion, salt and pepper, then mix together well.

Lay out 16 slices of bread and butter them. Place equal amounts of the chicken mix on 8 of the slices, spread it around evenly then top each sandwich with its buttered partner.

Carefully cut the crusts off (save these to feed to the ducks at the pond), then slice each sandwich into 3 fingers. Arrange these on a serving platter then cover with damp paper towels or a clean, damp tea towel until serving — this stops the sandwiches from drying out.

MAKES 24 FINGER SANDWICHES, 2 PER PERSON

Pecan crunch cookies are a recipe passed down from my lovely mum. When I started cooking with healthier ingredients I missed having these in my life, so I ended up giving Mum's treat a little makeover with coconut oil instead of butter, coconut sugar in place of raw sugar and spelt flour in place of wheat flour. Now they are firmly back on rotation and I'm happy to say that Mum, and all the kids in the family, absolutely love them!

Pecan crunch cookies

DF / V

125 ml (4 fl oz/½ cup)
  coconut oil
80 g (2¾ oz/½ cup)
  coconut sugar
2 tablespoons maple syrup
1 egg, beaten
110 g (3¾ oz/1 cup)
  spelt flour
90 g (3¼ oz/1 cup)
  desiccated coconut
50 g (1¾ oz/½ cup) rolled
  (porridge) oats
1 teaspoon aluminium-
  and gluten-free baking
  powder
24 pecan halves

Preheat the oven to 150°C (300°F) and line two baking trays (sheets) with baking paper.

Melt the coconut oil in a small saucepan on a low heat, then add the coconut sugar and maple syrup and whisk continuously for about 2–3 minutes, or until the sugar has completely dissolved.

Take the saucepan off the heat and stir through the egg followed by the spelt flour, coconut, oats and baking powder. Mix all the ingredients together well.

Measure out heaped teaspoons of the cookie mixture and roll these gently in your clean hands. Place them on the trays, leaving them enough room to spread out as they cook. Top each cookie with a pecan half. Bake for 20 minutes at the top of the oven. Once golden, allow to cool on the trays for 10 minutes, then either serve right away or store in an airtight container for up to 1 week.

MAKES 24 COOKIES, 2 PER PERSON

When I first started my business, The Brown Paper Bag, I had a stall at Bondi Beach's Saturday Growers' Market. These raw carrot cakes were a permanent fixture on my market menu. They are a divine mouthful of carrot and spices with a wonderful textural nutty crunch. Watching people eat them after they bought them from the stall was awesome. Their eyes would light up and they'd be back the next week for more, and to ask for the recipe. So here it is!

Raw carrot cakes

GF / DF / SF / V / VG

1 kg (2 lb 4 oz) carrots, peeled and grated
250 g (9 oz) Medjool dates, pitted
175 g (6 oz) organic Turkish apricots
85 g (3 oz) walnut halves
150 g (5½ oz/2¼ cups) shredded coconut
115 g (4 oz/¾ cup) currants
1 teaspoon ground cinnamon
1 teaspoon ground nutmeg
cashew or almond butter (softened), to serve

Put the grated carrots in a large bowl. Combine the dates, apricots and walnuts in a food processor and pulse until a fine crumb is achieved. Don't whizz them too much; you have to be careful not to let this mix turn to a paste, as a crunchy texture is important to the final experience.

Add the date mixture to the carrots in the bowl, followed by the coconut, currants and spices. Using clean hands, bring all the ingredients together to form the cake mix. Again, don't overwork the mix — just bring the ingredients together.

Measure out 2 heaped tablespoons (¼ cup) of the cake mixture and shape it with your hands to form a cube or little ball. Repeat until you have used up the rest of the mixture. Place these on squares of baking paper, then arrange on a tray.

Once all of the cakes are made, top each with a spoonful of nut butter and then put them in the fridge to firm up for at least 1 hour. Store and eat the cakes straight from the fridge. They will keep for up to 1 week.

MAKES 24 CAKES, 2 PER PERSON

RAW CARROT CAKES

ICED DANDELION TEA
recipe page 51

Almond meal makes a wonderful substitute for wheat flour in sweet and savoury pastries. The fat in the almonds holds together to give a lovely 'short' pastry experience while also nourishing your body with some good-quality essential fats, which stabilise blood sugar and energy levels.

Passionfruit shortbreads

GF / DF / SF / V

Shortbread

200 g (7 oz/2 cups) almond meal

2 tablespoons coconut oil, melted

4 tablespoons rice malt syrup

a generous pinch of sea salt

2 pinches of vanilla powder or 1 teaspoon vanilla extract or paste

Passionfruit curd

3 tablespoons lemon juice

3 tablespoons strained passionfruit pulp

2 eggs

2 extra egg yolks

3 tablespoons maple syrup

4 tablespoons coconut oil

Serve with a few thin strips of lemon zest (optional)

To make the shortbread, preheat the oven to 180°C (350°F) and line a baking tray (baking sheet) with baking paper. Combine all of the ingredients for the shortbread in a small bowl and mix with a wooden spoon until a dough is formed. Using a small spoon, scoop spoonfuls of dough, roll them gently in your hands, then flatten them gently into rounds on the baking tray. Bake in the oven for 7–10 minutes, or until lightly golden. Keep checking to ensure they don't burn. Remove from the oven, then allow to cool for 10 minutes on the baking tray.

To make the passionfruit curd, place a small stainless-steel bowl over a small saucepan of simmering water, ensuring the base of the bowl isn't touching the water. Turn the heat down to low. Pour in the lemon juice, passionfruit pulp, eggs, extra egg yolks and maple syrup, whisking with electric beaters until combined. Gradually whisk in the coconut oil, a tablespoon at a time, until it is completely melted.

Increase the heat to medium, continuing to whisk. The mixture should gradually become thicker until a curd consistency forms. At this point, remove the bowl from the saucepan and set aside to cool completely. Place in the fridge to allow the curd to set and become firmer.

Dollop spoonfuls of passionfruit curd on top of each shortbread, adding a delicate strip of lemon zest for decoration if you like, then serve.

MAKES 24, 2 PER PERSON

Photograph page 40

Iced dandelion tea

GF / DF / SF / V / VG

Dandelion root is bitter in flavour and not dissimilar to the taste of coffee. The bitterness stimulates the liver and the body's elimination pathways. This tea can also be enjoyed without coconut milk, but it does make the end result taste delightfully decadent!

6 dandelion tea bags
1 teaspoon vanilla powder or
* ¼ teaspoon vanilla extract or paste*
2 tablespoons maple syrup (optional)
500 ml (17 fl oz/2 cups) coconut milk
Serve with ice cubes

Steep the dandelion tea bags in a large ceramic jug or glass beverage dispenser filled with 1.8 litres (64 fl oz) of boiling water for 20 minutes. Remove the tea bags, then stir through the vanilla and maple syrup until the vanilla powder dissolves. Chill in the fridge for 30 minutes.

   Once chilled, pour into 12 glasses, drop in some ice cubes and finish with about 2 tablespoons of coconut milk per person.

SERVES 12

Photograph page 49

White peach and banana smoothie

GF / DF / SF / V

Hemp seeds have a wonderful amino acid profile, providing a great source of protein in this smoothie. If hemp isn't available, then rice protein, pea protein or a simple raw egg (see note below) are all great options if you want to increase the protein.

4 white peaches
2 bananas
1 litre (35 fl oz/4 cups) rice milk
1½ tablespoons honey
1½ tablespoons hemp seeds
1½ tablespoons camu powder

Blend all of the ingredients together until smooth and serve to your guests in little shot glasses upon their arrival.

NOTE

Raw egg should never be consumed by pregnant women, the elderly, or anyone with a compromised immune system. Only use it in this smoothie if it's for your own consumption, or if you have confirmed that it's OK with your guests beforehand.

SERVES 12

Photograph page 40

You might be surprised to learn that the nutritional profile of this caramel slice is incredibly diverse. The nuts and seeds used here are rich in omega-3 and amino acids, there is just the right amount of natural sweetness with a hint of vanilla, and the delicious clean caramel gets a touch of endocrine support courtesy of the maca powder. This can be made well ahead of time and stored in the freezer for up to two weeks.

Raw almond caramel slice

GF / DF / SF / V / VG

Base

60 g (2¼ oz/½ cup) walnut halves
40 g (1½ oz/¼ cup) almonds
125 g (4½ oz) Medjool dates,
 pitted (approximately 7 dates)
2 tablespoons coconut oil,
 melted
3 tablespoons raw cacao
 powder
1 tablespoon linseeds
1 tablespoon chia seeds
2 tablespoons rice malt syrup

Raw caramel

70 g (2½ oz/¼ cup)
 almond butter
2 tablespoons hulled tahini
2 tablespoons rice malt syrup
75 g (2¾ oz) Medjool dates,
 pitted (approximately 4 dates)
2 teaspoons vanilla paste
 or extract
1 teaspoon maca powder
115 g (4 oz/¾ cup) chopped
 almonds

Chocolate topping

3 tablespoons coconut oil
3 tablespoons rice malt syrup
3 tablespoons raw cacao powder

Combine all of the base ingredients in a food processor and blitz to a crumb, or until a paste is formed if you prefer a smoother texture for your base. If you need to loosen the ingredients to assist with blending, add a touch of water.

Line a square 20 cm (8 inch) cake tin with baking paper, then spoon the base mixture into the tin and evenly spread it around. Place in the freezer while you prepare the caramel and topping.

Place all of the raw caramel ingredients, except the chopped almonds, in the food processor and blitz until a smooth caramel-like texture forms. Take the base out of the freezer and spread the caramel evenly over the surface. Sprinkle over half of the chopped almonds, then return to the freezer.

To finish the slice, make the chocolate topping by melting the coconut oil in a small saucepan on a low heat. Once the oil has melted, remove from the heat and add the rice malt syrup and cacao powder. Whisk well to create a smooth melted chocolate. Pour this molten chocolate over the slice, then spread it out evenly over the top and finish by sprinkling over the remaining chopped almonds.

Return to the freezer and allow to set for approximately 4–6 hours. Serve straight from the freezer.

MAKES 24 SLICES, 2 PER PERSON

light lunch

Eating light is a key component of spring. By the time winter comes to an end, many of us have probably indulged in more heavy food and late nights than we should have, so by spring we're ready for some daylight nourishment. Eating lighter foods in the middle of warmer days often works better for our energy levels.

For spring lunches, an even balance of warm cooked foods and cool raw foods is the best approach. Be sure to focus on integrating clean proteins such as organic chicken or fish (salmon, trout, barramundi) teamed with fresh salads and steamed greens with an accompaniment of grains.

SERVES 4

MAINS

BAKED SALMON
WITH HORSERADISH
YOGHURT

SPRING VEGETABLE
QUINOA RISOTTO

SIDES

ROSEMARY
CHICKPEA BREAD

CUCUMBER RIBBONS,
GOAT'S CHEESE AND
DILL SALAD WITH
AVOCADO DRESSING

STEAMED SPRING
VEGETABLES

SPROUTED QUINOA
TABBOULEH

DRINK

TURMERIC TEA

Everyone has a comfort food or a favourite meal, and salmon is mine. This baked salmon in particular ticks all the boxes: it highlights the delicious nature of the fish, has just a hint of zing from the sumac, and the creamy horseradish yoghurt sets off a flavour explosion with every bite. So good.

Baked salmon with horseradish yoghurt

GF / SF

a side of salmon
(approximately
1 kg/2 lb 4 oz), skin on
and pinboned
sea salt
2 tablespoons
ground sumac
Lemon slices, to serve

Horseradish yoghurt
260 g (9¼ oz/1 cup)
Greek-style yoghurt
2 tablespoons finely grated
horseradish, either fresh
or from a jar
2 tablespoons finely
chopped chives
freshly ground black
pepper

Preheat the oven to 200°C (400°F). Get a large baking tray (baking sheet) and place a piece of foil about double the size of the tray on it. Place a large piece of baking paper on top of the foil, then lay the salmon, skin side down, on the tray. Season with salt and then rub the sumac all over the flesh. Bring the baking paper over the salmon and fold at the edges to completely enclose it. Bring the ends of the foil together over the top to double-seal the salmon and create a parcel.

Bake in the oven for 25 minutes then remove and allow to rest, still in the parcel, for 8–10 minutes.

While the salmon is resting, prepare the horseradish yoghurt. Whisk together the yoghurt, horseradish and chives, then season well with salt and pepper, to taste.

Unwrap the salmon and carefully transfer it to a serving platter (move it on the paper, then trim around it if you like). Garnish with lemon slices and serve next to a small bowl of the horseradish yoghurt. Any leftover horseradish yoghurt will keep for a couple of days in the fridge — it goes really well with the rare roast beef on page 104.

SERVES 4

Nutritional yeast is rich in B vitamins and also happens to be a wonderful non-dairy, vegan substitute for cheese in risottos. You will find nutritional yeast at your local health-food store. If you don't have any on hand and prefer cheese, then approximately half a cup of shaved parmesan or pecorino is perfect in this recipe.

Spring vegetable quinoa risotto

GF / DF / SF / V / VG

1 tablespoon coconut oil

2 leeks, white parts only, finely sliced

4 garlic cloves, finely chopped

1 small fennel bulb, roughly diced, frondy tops reserved for garnish

400 g (14 oz/2 cups) quinoa, rinsed and drained

1.25 litres (44 fl oz/5 cups) vegetable stock

700 g (1 lb 9 oz/2 large bunches) asparagus, woody ends trimmed and discarded, spears cut into thirds

4 kale leaves, stalks removed, leaves roughly torn

280 g (10 oz/2 cups) fresh or frozen peas

4 tablespoons nutritional yeast

90 g ($3\frac{1}{4}$ oz/2 cups) baby spinach leaves, loosely packed

sea salt and freshly ground black pepper, to taste

a small handful of flat-leaf (Italian) parsley leaves

Place a large saucepan on a medium heat and melt the coconut oil. Once melted, add the leek, stir, then reduce the heat to low and cook for approximately 5 minutes, or until the leek is transparent. Add the garlic and fennel and cook for a further 4–5 minutes, stirring frequently to ensure the ingredients do not stick to the base of the saucepan.

Add the quinoa and allow to cook (without any liquid) for 3–4 minutes, or until the grains become slightly golden in colour. Once you can see that tinge of colour, add 500 ml (17 fl oz/2 cups) of stock and stir to combine. Be sure to keep the lid off of the saucepan at all times throughout cooking or the quinoa will cook too quickly. Allow the liquid to be absorbed before adding another

500 ml of stock and continue stirring until it is almost absorbed.

As you start to see the tails of the quinoa appear, add the asparagus, kale leaves, and pour in the last 250 ml of stock. Cook for a further 2–3 minutes.

Stir the peas through the risotto and cook for another 1 minute then remove the pan from the heat and add the nutritional yeast and baby spinach. Stir these ingredients into the risotto. The aim is to keep the greens vibrant in colour, so be careful not to add your peas and spinach too early. Season with salt and pepper, then divide between your serving bowls. Garnish with the parsley and the reserved fennel tops, then serve.

SERVES 4

Chickpea bread, or socca as it is also known, is a delicious accompaniment to meals, boosting the protein and plant-based nutrition. It can be baked, as I've done here, or poured into a large skillet or lightly oiled frying pan and cooked on the stove until golden and puffed up.

Rosemary chickpea bread

GF / DF / SF / V / VG

130 g (4¾ oz/1 cup) besan
  (chickpea) flour
3 tablespoons grapeseed
  or olive oil
½ teaspoon sea salt
5 rosemary sprigs,
  roughly chopped

Preheat the oven to 180°C (350°F) and line a 20 cm (8 inch) square baking tin with baking paper.

Combine the besan with 250 ml (9 fl oz/1 cup) of water, the oil and salt in a food processor and blitz until the mixture is smooth and resembles batter. Add the rosemary to the mixture and blitz again. Pour into the baking tin and bake in the oven for 35 minutes.

Allow to cool in the tin for approximately 5–10 minutes before serving.

MAKES 1 FLAT LOAF, TO SERVE 4–6

This is one of my favourite salads to serve when I'm feeding a crowd. Cucumber ribbons are a delightful alternative to chopped salads and the goat's cheese offers a heavenly creamy flavour to the dish. Goat's cheese is often more easily digested than regular cheese as it contains less lactose than cow's milk.

Cucumber ribbons, goat's cheese and dill salad with avocado dressing

GF / SF / V

3 Lebanese cucumbers

2 tablespoons pepitas
 (pumpkin seeds)

2 tablespoons sunflower
 seeds

40 g (1½ oz/¼ cup) finely
 chopped red onion

35 g (1¼ oz/1 cup, firmly
 packed) rocket (arugula)
 or watercress leaves

a small handful of
 dill

75 g (2¾ oz) goat's cheese

sea salt and freshly
 ground black pepper

1 teaspoon white
 balsamic vinegar

Avocado dressing

1 avocado, peeled, destoned
 and mashed until smooth

1 teaspoon finely grated
 lime zest

a pinch of sea salt

1 teaspoon lime juice

To make the avocado dressing, whisk together all the ingredients by hand or with a food processor until smooth.

To make the salad, finely shave the cucumber lengthways using a mandolin or wide vegetable peeler. Arrange half of the cucumber slices on a serving platter or salad bowl, add a few small dollops of the avocado dressing, then top with half of the pepitas, sunflower seeds, onion, rocket and dill, then crumble over the goat's cheese.

Do the same again to create a lovely second layer in the salad. Season with salt and pepper, to taste, then add a drizzle of white balsamic and serve.

SERVES 4

Be careful not to overcook your steamed vegetables; set a timer so you keep on top of this. It's always better to pull them out a little early and have some crunch left in them than to leave them and find they've lost their colour and crispness.

Steamed spring vegetables

GF / DF / SF / V / VG

1 fennel bulb, sliced,
   frondy tops reserved
4 silverbeet (Swiss chard)
   leaves
65 g (2¼ oz/½ cup) fresh
   or frozen baby peas
45 g (1¾ oz/1 cup) baby
   spinach leaves
1 tablespoon extra virgin
   olive oil
½ a lemon
sea salt and freshly
   ground black pepper

Bring a large saucepan of water to the boil and check that a large steamer basket can sit comfortably over the pan without touching the water. Alternatively, you can place a sieve over a saucepan of boiling water (making sure the water doesn't touch the sieve).

Drop the sliced fennel into the steamer basket, cover with the lid, then cook for 5 minutes. Add the silverbeet and peas, cover and steam for a further minute.

Remove the vegetables from the steamer and arrange them on a plate with the baby spinach and reserved fennel tops. Season with the extra virgin olive oil, a good squeeze of lemon juice and some salt and pepper, then serve immediately.

SERVES 4

You will need to start this recipe three days in advance in order to sprout the quinoa. This might sound like a lot of work, but it really is very easy to do and it's well worth the effort because sprouting is an incredible means of amplifying the nutrition in seeds and nuts. However, if your schedule doesn't allow for sprouting, using regular cooked quinoa is completely fine. Cooked buckwheat also works well in this tabbouleh in place of the more traditional cracked wheat.

Sprouted quinoa tabbouleh

GF / DF / SF / V / VG

100 g ($3\frac{1}{2}$ oz/$\frac{1}{2}$ cup) quinoa

140 g (5 oz) baby or cherry tomatoes, quartered

100 g ($3\frac{1}{2}$ oz) red capsicum (pepper), roughly diced

2 tablespoons finely diced red onion

a handful of finely chopped flat-leaf (Italian) parsley leaves and stalks (approximately $\frac{1}{2}$ a bunch)

a small handful of finely chopped coriander (cilantro) leaves and stalks (approximately $\frac{1}{4}$ of a bunch)

a small handful of finely chopped mint leaves (approximately $\frac{1}{4}$ of a bunch)

1 tablespoon finely chopped red banana chilli, or to taste

1 tablespoon extra virgin olive oil

sea salt and freshly ground black pepper

1 lemon

Three days before you want to make the tabbouleh, rinse the quinoa under cold running water then put it in a large jar and fill the jar with water. Put the lid on. Leave to stand on the kitchen counter for 24 hours, rinsing two or three times during this period. Once the quinoa has finished soaking, drain all of the water and rinse it one final time.

Place a double layer of paper towels on a large tray and scatter over the quinoa in an even layer. Place the tray in a reasonably well-lit area of the kitchen or dining room and leave to sprout for 24 hours. Change the paper towels once during the sprouting process.

You'll know the quinoa has sprouted when the tails have grown out of the grain. Store your sprouted quinoa in a glass jar in the fridge for up to 3 days.

To make the salad, combine all of the salad ingredients and quinoa sprouts in a medium-sized serving bowl. Drizzle the extra virgin olive oil over the top. Season with salt and pepper, add the juice of half the lemon and toss lightly. Cut the other lemon half into wedges and serve the tabbouleh with your choice of chicken, meat, fish or legumes and lemon wedges for squeezing over.

SERVES 4 AS A SIDE

Turmeric tea is warming and grounding, so it's often one I bring out on the cooler days in early spring. It's like a big internal hug when you're feeling unsettled. The portions are small here as the combination of coconut milk and turmeric is quite rich, so aim to serve it in petite teacups if you have some on hand. Turmeric is useful because it reduces the symptoms (and risk of developing) inflammatory conditions of the gut and cardiovascular system. Aim to make it a regular part of your diet and serve it with a fat (coconut milk, egg yolk or avocado are great) to help your body access turmeric's powerful compound, curcumin.

Turmeric tea

GF / DF / SF / V

500 ml (9 fl oz/2 cups)
  coconut milk
2 teaspoons ground
  turmeric (or a 2 cm/
  $\frac{3}{4}$ inch piece of turmeric
  root, finely grated)
1 teaspoon ground
  cinnamon, plus extra
  to serve
$\frac{1}{2}$ teaspoon ground
  cardamom
2 cloves
a pinch of sea salt
raw honey, to serve

In a small saucepan, combine the coconut milk, spices and salt. Bring the ingredients to a very gentle simmer and continue to simmer for 5 minutes.

Remove from the heat and serve with an extra sprinkle of cinnamon and a drizzle of honey.

SERVES 4

spring picnic

When the days are still fresh and slowly warming up, I love celebrating the outdoors, and picnics are the perfect way to combine food with a bit of movement. Our bodies are naturally kept quieter during the winter as we tend to spend most of our time indoors. By the time spring rolls around, that urge to be outside in the fresh air has been building — and a picnic is a great way to satisfy that need to get moving at a park, by the sea or somewhere you enjoy spending time.

When putting together a picnic menu, think about foods that can be picked up easily and eaten by hand, as this will lighten your load of utensils (and washing up after!). Better still, create more substantial items that use beautiful plant foods as the utensils, such as grilled or shredded chicken rolled up in leaves of silverbeet, lettuce or cabbage, or little pastry shells made from chickpea flour and filled with roast pumpkin or tomato and goat's cheese. A few small bunches of spring blooms tied with twine and placed around the picnic table or blanket will bring the scene to life and make it that extra bit special.

SERVES 4

GRAZE

SEED SNAPS

BAKED HERB RICOTTA

FRESH PRAWNS
WITH DILL MAYONNAISE

OLIVE AND BROCCOLI
TAPENADE

BEETROOT HUMMUS

SAVOURY

SHREDDED CHICKEN
IN CABBAGE CUPS

BESAN TARTS WITH TOMATO,
GOAT'S CHEESE AND MINT

SPRING VEGETABLE
FRITTATA

SWEET

RAW CITRUS CAMU BALLS

MAPLE SPELT CUPCAKES

BANANA AND
COCONUT BREAD

DRINKS

POMEGRANATE, ORANGE
AND MINT SPRITZER

Seed snaps are a staple in our home. They are incredibly versatile accompaniments for both savoury and sweet foods, and work well with canapés or as part of a larger lunch, to replace bread. Linseeds are one of the richest plant sources of omega-3 fatty acids, which are essential for brain and heart health, joint mobility and immunity. Soaking the linseeds before using them creates a gelatinous substance that acts as a beautiful binder in foods such as breads and these snaps. By soaking them we also activate or unlock their nutrients, giving our bodies greater access to them.

Seed snaps

GF / DF / SF / V / VG

140 g (5 oz/1 cup) linseeds (flaxseeds)
100 g (3½ oz) chia seeds
70 g (2½ oz/½ cup) sunflower seeds
40 g (1½ oz/¼ cup) sesame seeds
40 g (1½ oz/¼ cup) pepitas (pumpkin seeds)
¼ teaspoon sea salt
2 tablespoons coconut oil, melted

Combine the linseeds with 375 ml (13 fl oz/1½ cups) of water in a bowl and allow to gel for 30 minutes.

Place the other seeds in a large bowl with the salt and mix. Add the linseed gel and the coconut oil, then mix again to ensure all of the seeds are distributed evenly through the mixture.

Line a 25 × 38 cm (10 × 15 inch) baking tray (baking sheet) with baking paper and spread the seed mixture evenly around the tray. Set aside for about 30 minutes so all the ingredients can sort of 'glue' together.

Preheat the oven to 160°C (315°F). Pop the tray in the oven and bake for 30 minutes, then remove from the oven and carefully turn the entire seed snap over. Score the snap evenly using a sharp knife so it is easier to break apart later. You want to get about 40 snaps from one tray (cut them smaller if using for canapés).

Return the tray to the oven and bake for a further 40 minutes, or until crisp. Allow to cool on the tray then break into pieces.

TIP

These snaps are great for picnics and lunchboxes and also make a tasty quick snack on the run. A batch of snaps should last for up to 2 weeks in an airtight container.

MAKES 40 SNAPS

BAKED HERB RICOTTA
recipe page 72

SEED SNAPS

Baked herb ricotta

GF / SF / V

Baked cheese is utterly decadent, but ricotta is a slightly healthier althernative to, say, brie or camembert, which are often served warm and oozing, with crackers. My version is lighter, and it is served cold rather than out of the oven, but it's still such a treat and always goes quickly.

360 g (12¾ oz) full-fat ricotta cheese
2 eggs
good pinch of sea salt
45 g (1¾ oz/¼ cup) Kalamata olives, pitted
  and roughly chopped (optional)
a handful of mixed soft herb leaves (basil, parsley
  and dill are beautiful with this), finely chopped
2 teaspoons olive oil

Preheat the oven to 180°C (350°F) and line a 7 × 25 cm (2¾ × 10 inch) loaf (bar) tin with baking paper. If you don't have a loaf tin, an ovenproof ceramic dish will also work.

Whisk together the ricotta, eggs and salt, then spoon half of this mixture into the loaf tin. Scatter over the olives and herbs, then spoon over the remaining ricotta mixture.

Brush the top of the ricotta with olive oil and bake for 1 hour and 15 minutes, or until the ricotta is cooked and is a beautiful golden colour on top.

Allow to cool for 30 minutes, then refrigerate for at least 1 hour prior to serving, or the night before if you want to get really organised. Remove from the tin and serve cut into thick slices with some of the seed snaps on the previous page.

SERVES 4

Photograph page 71

Fresh prawns with dill mayonnaise

GF / DF / SF

Set the tone for your picnic by pulling out this platter of prawns and dill mayo as soon as you arrive. Not only is it a lovely light dish to start with, but it also ensures the seafood and mayonnaise are eaten straight away while they are still nicely chilled and at their absolute best.

600 g (1 lb 5 oz) king prawns, cooked, peeled
  and deveined (tails left on)
juice of ½ a lemon
2 tablespoons finely chopped chives
sea salt and freshly ground black pepper
lemon halves, for serving

Dill mayonnaise
235 g (8½ oz/1 cup) good-quality
  whole-egg mayonnaise
2 tablespoons finely chopped dill
1 tablespoon lemon juice

To make the dill mayonnaise, simply whisk together all of the ingredients, add salt and pepper to taste, then place in a small serving bowl and refrigerate until needed.

In a large bowl, toss the cooked prawns with the lemon juice and chives, then season well with salt and pepper. Keep chilled until needed, then arrange the prawns on a platter next to the dill mayo and a lemon half.

SERVES 4

FRESH PRAWNS WITH
DILL MAYONNAISE

Olive and broccoli tapenade

GF / DF / SF / V / VG

When people ask me what my vice is, I don't always have one to offer. However, recently as I've pondered things I love to taste (and share), I've realised the salty juiciness of olives is up there on my list. So it seems fitting to have this beautiful olive dip to share at a picnic. The best thing about this one is the addition of raw broccoli, which supercharges the tapenade with wonderful phytochemicals. So, if this is my one vice, it's not a bad one to have.

60 g (2¼ oz/1 cup) broccoli florets
175 g (6 oz/1 cup) green olives, pitted
1 small garlic clove, crushed
2 tablespoons capers in brine, drained and rinsed
1 teaspoon camu powder
3 tablespoons extra virgin olive oil
freshly ground black pepper

Place the broccoli florets in a food processor and blitz until a crumb or rice-like consistency is achieved.

Add the rest of the ingredients to the processor and blitz again until you have a nice, slightly chunky, uniform texture.

Store in an airtight glass jar in the fridge for up to 1 week.

MAKES 400 ML (14 OZ)

Spring vegetable frittata

GF / DF / SF / V

A frittata is such an easy dish to take along to a picnic, and I love this one with its pretty spring colours and green veggies popping out. A bonus is that you can make it the night before and keep it in the fridge until you are ready to walk out the door.

1 tablespoon grapeseed oil
1 small red onion, finely diced
40 g (1½ oz/¼ cup) fresh or frozen peas
1 zucchini (courgette), sliced thinly lengthways
160 g (5¾ oz/1 bunch) asparagus, woody ends
   trimmed and discarded, spears cut into thirds
8 eggs
a small handful of basil leaves, finely sliced
sea salt and freshly ground black pepper

Preheat the oven grill (broiler) to medium–high.

Heat the oil in a medium ovenproof frying pan over a medium heat. Add the onion and sauté for 5 minutes, or until translucent. Add the peas, zucchini and asparagus, cover with a lid and cook for 3–4 minutes.

Meanwhile, whisk together the eggs, basil leaves and a few good pinches of salt and pepper in a large bowl.

Give the vegetables a gentle stir to spread them evenly around the pan. Pour the egg mixture all over the vegetables, then cover and leave to cook for another 6–8 minutes; the top will still have some liquid egg at this stage.

Place the frying pan under the grill to cook for a further 5–6 minutes, or until the frittata is golden and puffed up. Allow to cool in the pan for 10 minutes before slicing and serving.

SERVES 4-6

SPRING VEGETABLE
FRITTATA

Hummus always goes down well at picnics and for nibbles, but the addition of beetroot really gives this one a lift. I love creating a rainbow of colours with food to entice the eye and draw people in, so beetroot is often one of my go-to's. I really believe that digestion starts the minute you engage with food, so create beautiful healthy food that is eye-catching as well as tasty, and it will all flow well from there!

Beetroot hummus

GF / DF / SF / V / VG

2 tablespoons grapeseed oil

1 large beetroot (beet), peeled and grated (see note)

400 g (14 oz) cooked chickpeas (drained and rinsed well if from a tin)

1 small garlic clove, crushed

3 tablespoons extra virgin olive oil

1 teaspoon ground cumin

$\frac{1}{2}$ teaspoon sweet paprika

3 tablespoons lemon juice

2 tablespoons hulled tahini

$\frac{1}{2}$ teaspoon finely grated horseradish, either fresh or from a jar, or 2 horseradish leaves, finely chopped

$\frac{1}{2}$ teaspoon sea salt

freshly ground black pepper

Warm the grapeseed oil in a frying pan over a medium heat then add the grated beetroot. Cook for approximately 6–7 minutes, tossing frequently.

Place the chickpeas, garlic, olive oil, cumin, paprika, lemon juice and tahini in a food processor and blend until combined.

Add the cooked beetroot, horseradish, salt and a few grinds of pepper to the chickpea mixture with 3 tablespoons of water, then blend until smooth.

Store in an airtight glass jar in the fridge for up to 1 week.

NOTE

Use gloves when grating the beetroot if you don't want bright red hands!

MAKES 400 G (14 OZ)

Shredded chicken in cabbage cups

GF / DF / SF

1 large skinless chicken breast (approx. 200 g/7 oz)
1 carrot, julienned
2 red radishes, trimmed and julienned
2 spring onions (scallions), white part only,
   finely sliced
190 g (6¾ oz/1 cup) finely sliced pineapple
a very large handful of mint leaves
a very large handful of coriander (cilantro) leaves,
   stalks finely chopped
40 g (1½ oz/¼ cup) almonds, toasted and
   roughly chopped
400 g (14 oz) red cabbage, leaves separated
   and trimmed to form triangular cups

Dressing
3 tablespoons lime juice
2 tablespoons tamari
2 tablespoons maple syrup
2 teaspoons fish sauce
½ a bird's eye chilli, seeds removed, finely chopped

Bring a small saucepan of water to the boil. Place
the chicken breast in the water, bring back to the
boil, then immediately turn off the heat, cover
with a lid and leave to poach for 30 minutes.

Once the chicken is cooked, take it out of the
water and allow it to cool while you prepare
the salad dressing.

Whisk all of the dressing ingredients together.

Shred the chicken into fine pieces and toss
with the remaining ingredients in a serving bowl
(except the cabbage). Pour the dressing over the
chicken mixture, then toss to combine.

To serve, place the cabbage leaves on a platter
surrounding the bowl of chicken filling. Have
guests fill their own cabbage leaves and eat!

MAKES 16 CABBAGE CUPS, TO SERVE 4

Pomegranate, orange and mint spritzer

GF / DF / SF / V / VG

It's so great to have healthy soft-drink
options — ones that avoid refined sugars
and have yummy bursts of fruit flavours —
available at picnics and other events. I love
lemon, lime and mint combinations, but
berries also work a treat. Slice the fruit up
in advance and simply add to bottles of
sparkling water, or mix together in a jug
once you get there. Pretty *and* refreshing.

2 litres (70 fl oz/8 cups) sparkling mineral water
2 oranges, halved and finely sliced
1 lemon, halved and finely sliced
1 lime, halved and finely sliced
2 large handfuls of mint leaves
seeds from 1 pomegranate

Combine all of the ingredients in a large water jug
(or beverage dispenser if you want to add a bit of
elegance to your picnic and you have helpers!)
and stir gently. Allow the flavours to infuse for
20 minutes before serving. Add ice, if you like.

SERVES 4

Besan flour has a beautiful nutty flavour and is a great option for those who are gluten intolerant or looking for alternatives to traditional flours in pastries, tarts and other baked goodies.
It is made from ground chickpeas, which are a wonderful source of plant-based protein and insoluble fibre. Increasing the amount of plant-based protein sources in our diet is beneficial for everyone, especially anyone trying to manage their weight, improve muscle recovery and repair or control blood sugar levels.

Besan tarts with tomato, goat's cheese and mint

GF / SF / V

Besan pastry

180 g (6 oz/1½ cups) besan (chickpea) flour

65 g (2¼ oz/½ cup) coconut flour

1 teaspoon sea salt

4 tablespoons olive oil

Tart filling

100 g (3½ oz) goat's cheese, crumbled

½ a small red onion, finely diced

350 g (12 oz) baby roma tomatoes, diced

sea salt and freshly ground black pepper

a small handful of mint leaves, finely shredded

To make the pastry, preheat the oven to 180°C (350°F). In a food processor, combine both flours with the salt and blitz briefly. With the blade moving, slowly start pouring in the olive oil and 125 ml (4 fl oz/½ cup) of water. You should see a sticky dough start to form. You may need to add a little extra coconut flour if the dough feels too wet.

Transfer the dough to your work surface and halve it. Place one of the halves between two large pieces of baking paper. Using a rolling pin, roll it out between the two sheets of baking paper until about 5 mm (¼ inch) thick. Repeat with the other half.

Using a 9 cm (3½ inch) cookie cutter, cut out 8 pastry circles and gently press these into the holes of a 125 ml (4 oz/½ cup) capacity patty pan. Line with baking paper and fill with pastry weights or uncooked rice and place in the oven for 15 minutes to blind bake. Remove from the oven, remove the pastry and weights and allow to cool.

Once cooled, fill the pastry cases by crumbling goat's cheese evenly into each one, followed by some onion and tomato and then season well. Finish with shreds of mint resting on top of each tart.

NOTE

Any extra tart shells can be frozen and will just need a quick flash in the oven before you serve them.

MAKES 8 LITTLE TARTS, 2 PER PERSON

Raw citrus camu balls

GF / DF / SF / V

You'll notice camu powder pops up in a fair few of my recipes, and for good reason: camu is a rich, beautiful little fruit from Peru that is incredibly high in phytochemicals and antioxidants, which protect cells from free-radical damage. It brings a lovely citrus flavour to these energy balls. There are unlikely to be any left over from the picnic, but you can make a double batch and store the other dozen in the fridge for up to two weeks, or in the freezer for up to four weeks. They are amazing little hits of energy when you are craving something sweet.

195 g (7 oz/1$\frac{1}{4}$ cups) cashews
55 g (2 oz/$\frac{3}{4}$ cups) shredded coconut
1 tablespoon raw honey
2 tablespoons lemon juice
2 tablespoons orange juice
1 teaspoon finely grated lemon zest
1 teaspoon finely grated orange zest
2 teaspoons camu powder
2 tablespoons desiccated coconut, for rolling

Combine the cashews and shredded coconut in a food processor and blitz to a fine crumb. Add the honey, citrus juices and zests and camu powder then blitz until a dough forms.

Measure 1 level tablespoon per ball, then roll between your palms and then in the desiccated coconut until completely coated. Place on a tray lined with baking paper and chill in the fridge to help them keep their shape a bit better.

MAKES 12 BALLS

Maple spelt cupcakes

SF / V

Cupcakes always get people excited at picnics and parties. These keep to tradition in flavour with just a few tweaks to the ingredients. I love icing these with nut butter or yoghurt, but even without they are still amazingly scrumptious.

150 g (5$\frac{1}{2}$ oz) unsalted butter, softened
3 tablespoons maple syrup
2 eggs
1 teaspoon aluminium- and gluten-free baking powder
$\frac{1}{2}$ teaspoon bicarbonate of soda (baking soda)
1 tablespoon vanilla paste or extract
170 g (6 oz/1$\frac{1}{2}$ cups) spelt flour
185 ml (6 fl oz/$\frac{3}{4}$ cup) milk

Serve with nut butter, crushed nuts or Greek-style yoghurt

Line 12 holes of a 250 ml (9 fl oz/1 cup) capacity cupcake tin with paper cases. Preheat the oven to 160°C (315°F).

Mix all of the ingredients together in a food processor, or with an electric hand-mixer, until well combined. Divide the batter between the holes and bake in the oven for 20 minutes. Leave to cool in the tin, then top with nut butter, crushed nuts or a dollop of yoghurt.

Any cupcakes left over after the picnic will freeze really well.

MAKES 12 CUPCAKES

RAW CITRUS CAMU BALLS

There's nothing quite like remaking an old favourite using new ideas and new ingredients, and this nourishing banana bread wins people over time after time, even though it's quite different from traditional banana bread. I've used dates to replace the refined sugars typically used for this, as well as a mixture of shredded coconut and brown rice flour in place of wheat flour. Spelt flour is also a great option if brown rice flour isn't on hand.

Banana and coconut bread

GF / DF / SF / V

125 ml (4 fl oz/$\frac{1}{2}$ cup)
   coconut oil, melted
1 teaspoon vanilla extract
   or vanilla paste
4 eggs, beaten
3 very ripe bananas,
   mashed
8 Medjool dates, pitted
   and chopped
1 teaspoon bicarbonate
   of soda (baking soda)
65 g (2$\frac{1}{4}$ oz/1 cup)
   shredded coconut
135 g (4$\frac{3}{4}$ oz/1 cup)
   brown rice flour

Preheat the oven to 180°C (350°F) and line a 10 x 22 cm (4 x 8$\frac{1}{2}$ inch) loaf (bar) tin with baking paper.

In a medium-sized bowl, mix the melted coconut oil with the vanilla, eggs, bananas, dates and bicarbonate of soda. Next, add the shredded coconut and brown rice flour and fold in until well combined.

Pour this mixture into the lined loaf tin and bake for approximately 45–60 minutes, or until a skewer inserted into the centre comes out clean.

Allow to cool in the tin for 10 minutes, then slice and pack up in a fresh piece of baking paper or brown paper with cotton twine to take to the picnic.

SERVES 8

summer

When I think of summer, it's sun, sand, bright colours, fun parties, breakfasts, barbecues and time spent on the beach that all spring to mind. Not in any particular order, but rather all merged into one incredible feeling for this season, when life goes into full throttle. Summer is the perfect time to balance life and nutrition with the rising and setting of the sun, making the most of the long days, with beach time aplenty and long summer nights spent with good friends and family. It's also a time when more of us take holidays so we can soak in a little more of this happiness.

Often, after people return from their summer holiday I'll hear them say they 'overdid' it by eating or drinking with a little too much gusto. Holidays don't have to feel that way. I'm a big believer in celebrating life, so the key to enjoying summer to its fullest is to create lovely meals that are balanced thanks to the right ingredients. As always, use seasonal fruits and vegetables, with an aim to include more raw nutrition in your life — this is the season for it. Raw food improves energy and health, helps to keep the body cool in a hot climate and creates a rainbow of food at the table.

SUMMER FRUITS
AVOCADO
BANANA
BERRIES
CHERRIES
CURRANTS
FIGS
GRAPES
LYCHEES
MANGO
NECTARINE
ORANGE
PASSIONFRUIT
PEAR
PINEAPPLE
PLUM

SUMMER VEGETABLES
ASPARAGUS
BORLOTTI BEANS
CAPSICUM (PEPPER)
CUCUMBER
DAIKON
EGGPLANT (AUBERGINE)
GREEN BEANS
LEEK
LETTUCE
RADISH
SNAKE BEANS
SNAP PEAS
SNOW PEAS (MANGE TOUT)
SPRING ONION (SCALLION)
SWEETCORN
TOMATO
WATERCRESS
ZUCCHINI (COURGETTE)

GRILLED STONE FRUIT AND
POMEGRANATE QUINOA

recipe page 92

breakfast by the beach

Over the years I've been lucky enough to edge my way up and down Sydney's coastline in the homes I've lived in, so beaches have always had a very strong presence in my life. I love the idea of waking up in the morning, having a run on the soft sand and a dip in the ocean, or even just seeing the water in the winter months. It's truly grounding and sets a day up so well. The next step to a perfect morning on the beach is, of course, one of the best meals of the day!

For a divinely nourishing breakfast, have a few smoothies on offer that are diverse in colour and flavour. These will bring a lovely element to the picnic table or blanket and are the perfect way to work in seasonal fruits and vegetables. When planning your breakfast menu, try to balance the textures of foods and keep in mind that crunch is a wonderful contrast to the smoothness of many traditional breakfast foods. A good toasty granola, some fresh raw vegetables or a delicious grain and seed bread will help introduce contrast as well as a wider variety of nutritional elements to the meal.

SERVES 4

DRINKS

SUMMER BERRY
BREAKFAST
SMOOTHIE

MANGO LASSI

SWEET MAINS

GRILLED STONE FRUIT
AND POMEGRANATE
QUINOA

BLUEBERRY AND
ALMOND MUFFINS

COCONUT GRANOLA

SAVOURY MAIN

GREEN PEA PANCAKES
WITH SMOKY TOMATO
SAUCE

SIDE

BUCKWHEAT
SEED BREAD

COCONUT GRANOLA (TOP LEFT) *recipe page 96*; MANGO LASSI (OPPOSITE) *recipe page 90*

Summer berry breakfast smoothie

GF / DF / SF / V

Probiotic powder has been added to this blend, which is something I'll often do in my smoothies. Simply crack open a probiotic capsule (which you can find in the fridge at most chemists and health-food stores), tip it into the mix and blend. Nothing like a little healthy bacteria to keep your gut flora in good nick.

150 g (5$\frac{1}{2}$ oz/1 cup) fresh or frozen berries
250 ml (9 fl oz/1 cup) almond milk
1 teaspoon raw honey
1 egg
1 tablespoon almond butter (or nut butter of choice)
1 teaspoon coconut oil
1 teaspoon or 1 capsule (broken, and contents added to mix) of probiotic powder (optional)

Combine all of the ingredients in a blender and blitz until smooth. Pour into jars with lids to take along to the beach. Shake gently right before serving.

MAKES 4 SMOOTHIE SHOTS OR TASTERS, OR SERVES 1

Mango lassi

GF / SF / V

Mangoes are a brilliant source of vitamin C for immune function and collagen formation; vitamin A and its supportive nutrients (beta-carotene, alpha carotene and beta-cryptoxanthin) for healthy skin; and potassium, which ensures optimum levels of fluid in your body. This lassi is a great way to kick off your day.

2 mango cheeks
70 g (2$\frac{1}{2}$ oz/$\frac{1}{4}$ cup) natural yoghurt
2 teaspoons camu powder

Combine all of the ingredients in a blender with 250 ml (9 fl oz/1 cup) of water and blitz until smooth. Pop into a jar with a lid and shake gently right before serving.

MAKES 4 SMOOTHIE SHOTS OR TASTERS, OR SERVES 1

Photograph page 89

SUMMER BERRY
BREAKFAST SMOOTHIE

If you're looking for a simple and fresh breakfast option or snack that really celebrates the stone fruits of the season, this is it. I use grilled nectarines or peaches to enrich the flavours; however the fresh fruits work supremely well, too. It's a great way of using up leftover quinoa — not a grain we use enough at breakfast, but I absolutely love its versatility in sweet or savoury dishes. Quinoa is particularly rich in plant protein to keep you feeling satisfied, energised and focused throughout the day.

Grilled stone fruit and pomegranate quinoa

GF / SF / V / VG OPTION / DF OPTION

3 peaches or nectarines, destoned and sliced thickly
3 teaspoons coconut oil, melted
225 g (8 oz/1½ cups) cooked quinoa
25 g (1 oz/½ cup) shredded coconut, toasted (optional)
190 g (6¾ oz/⅔ cup) Greek-style or coconut yoghurt
3 tablespoons pomegranate seeds
1½ tablespoons finely shredded mint leaves

Preheat your grill to high and line a baking tray (baking sheet) with baking paper.

Toss the stone fruit in the melted coconut oil, then arrange in a single layer on the baking tray. Place under the grill for approximately 12 minutes, or until the fruit is lightly golden.

While the fruit is grilling, toss the quinoa and coconut together and arrange in bowls. Top with grilled stone fruit, yoghurt, pomegranate and mint and serve.

SERVES 4

These beautiful muffins have been on rotation at my house for several years now. They really don't take long to make, and they come in so handy on mornings when you run out of time to have a sit-down breakfast. Kids also love them, and they're a much better breakfast option than many of the muffins found in shops and cafés, which often contain a lot of sugar. Make a batch of these, enjoy some of them warm from the oven and freeze the rest for easy breakfasts and snacks down the track.

Blueberry and almond muffins

GF / DF / SF / V

125 ml (4 fl oz/$\frac{1}{2}$ cup)
  coconut oil, melted
  (or butter, softened),
  and extra for greasing
  if needed
4 eggs, beaten
1 tablespoon maple syrup
2 teaspoons vanilla extract
1 teaspoon ground
  cinnamon
$\frac{1}{2}$ teaspoon gluten-
  and aluminium-free
  baking powder
a pinch of sea salt
1 large red apple, skin on,
  cored and grated
2 teaspoons finely grated
  lemon zest
100 g (3$\frac{1}{2}$ oz/1 cup)
  almond meal
55 g (2 oz/$\frac{1}{2}$ cup)
  coconut flour
235 g (8$\frac{1}{2}$ oz/1$\frac{1}{2}$ cups) fresh
  or frozen blueberries

Preheat the oven to 180°C (350°F) and line a 12-hole standard muffin tin with cases or lightly grease the holes.

Combine the melted coconut oil, eggs, maple syrup, vanilla, ground cinnamon, baking powder and salt in a large bowl and whisk well.

Add the grated apple, lemon zest, almond meal and coconut flour. Mix gently to combine, then lightly fold in half of the blueberries.

Spoon the mixture equally between the muffin cases and top with the remaining blueberries.

Bake in the oven for 25–30 minutes, or until golden on top, then remove and allow to cool in the tin for 15 minutes. These will keep in an airtight container for 3–4 days in the fridge, or can be frozen for 4 weeks.

MAKES 12 MUFFINS

Possibly one of the best granolas I've made in the history of my granola making, this is a recipe for the paleo, vegan, vegetarian, gluten-, dairy- and sugar-free lovers. It's full of nuts, seeds and coconut, and just the right amount of spices to allow the flavours of all the ingredients to shine. You won't need a huge serving; just a small amount will do as it contains healthy fats to make your stomach feel satiated.

Coconut granola

GF / DF / SF / V / VG

55 g (2 oz /1 cup)
  coconut flakes
80 g (2¾ oz/½ cup) almonds
80 g (2¾/½ cup) cashews
80 g (2¾ oz/½ cup) pepitas
  (pumpkin seeds)
75 g (2½ oz/½ cup)
  sunflower seeds
2 tablespoons chia seeds
½ teaspoon ground
  cinnamon
1 tablespoon maple syrup
2 tablespoons coconut
  oil, melted
60 g (2¼ oz/½ cup)
  goji berries
60 g (2¼ oz/½ cup)
  dried cherries

Optional spices (all
  ground): nutmeg,
  cardamom, ginger, cloves
  and vanilla powder

Preheat the oven to 180°C (350°F) and line a large baking tray (baking sheet) with baking paper.

Combine the coconut flakes, almonds, cashews, pepitas, sunflower seeds and chia seeds in a large bowl. Tip this mixture into a high-powered blender or food processor and pulse for about 10 seconds to chop slightly. You don't want the mix to become a crumb, so be careful not to look away and blend for too long. Tip the mixture back into the bowl.

In a separate bowl, combine the ground cinnamon, maple syrup and coconut oil and whisk lightly. Pour this mixture over the dry ingredients and toss to ensure everything is coated. Spread evenly around the baking tray and bake for 15 minutes.

Remove from the oven, add the goji berries and cherries and toss lightly. If you wish to add more spices at this stage, add small amounts and toss as you do so to ensure they are evenly distributed and the granloa does not end up 'over-spiced'.

Transfer to a wide jar or bowl and place on the table so everyone can help themselves. Save any leftovers in an airtight container for breakfast in the coming weeks. This will keep for up to 4 weeks.

SERVES 8, MAKES 450 G (1 LB)

Photograph page 88

The 'Life-Changing Loaf of Bread' recipe from Sarah Britton's blog, *My New Roots*, inspired this bread. I'm a huge fan of buckwheat and use it more frequently in my diet than most other grains. This bread is incredibly delicious fresh, but after day one it is best kept in the fridge where it lasts for up to one week. Alternatively, it can also be sliced and stored in the freezer for up to three weeks. Toasting the bread and spreading it with a healthy fat (such as mashed avocado, nut butter, ricotta or organic butter) makes the experience even better. You will need to start the prep for this recipe at least 8 hours before baking.

Buckwheat seed bread

GF / DF / SF / V / VG

270 g (9$\frac{1}{2}$ oz/1$\frac{1}{2}$ cups) buckwheat, soaked in water for 2 hours, then drained well (for approximately 20 minutes)

145 g (5 oz/1 cup) sunflower seeds

75 g (2$\frac{3}{4}$ oz/$\frac{1}{2}$ cup) pepitas (pumpkin seeds) or almonds

85 g (3 oz/$\frac{1}{2}$ cup) linseeds (flaxseeds)

1 tablespoon sesame seeds

2 tablespoons chia seeds

4 tablespoons psyllium husk

1 teaspoon sea salt

3 tablespoons coconut oil, melted

Optional: if you have any slippery elm on hand, you can also add 1 teaspoon of that to the dough

Line a 14 × 24 cm (5$\frac{1}{2}$ × 9$\frac{1}{2}$ inch) loaf (bar) tin or silicon loaf mould with baking paper.

In a large bowl, combine all of the ingredients and add 375 ml (13 fl oz/1$\frac{1}{2}$ cups) of water. Mix well to combine, then pour the mixture into the tin, and flatten with the back of a spoon so the loaf is even. Allow to sit for at least 2 hours, or overnight if you have left yourself enough time for this.

A few hours before you're ready to eat, preheat the oven to 160°C (315°F) and place the loaf in the middle of the oven. Bake for 1 hour, or until the top of the loaf has become nice and crisp.

Once cooked, flip the loaf upside down onto a wire baking rack and peel away the baking paper, if attached. Return to the oven on the rack and cook for a further hour, or until the loaf sounds hollow when tapped.

Allow to cool for at least 1 hour before slicing and serving.

MAKES 1 LOAF (YIELDING APPROXIMATELY 12 SLICES)

Photograph page 98

BUCKWHEAT
SEED BREAD
recipe page 97

GREEN PEA PANCAKES
SMOKY TOMATO SAUCE
recipes pages 100-101

One of my favourite Bondi haunts, Porch and Parlour, make these pancakes and they are the best, if not the only, green pea pancakes around. I love peas, always have and always will, so it's probably not surprising that these have become an essential item when I'm building the ultimate breakfast menu. Peas are sweet, juicy and a colourful delight — full of anti-inflammatory and antioxidant properties. These pancakes are also great with a poached or boiled egg if you want a great brekky at home, too.

Green pea pancakes

GF / DF OPTION / SF / V

Pancakes

280 g (10 oz/2 cups) frozen peas, blanched

$\frac{1}{2}$ a red onion, roughly chopped

juice and finely grated zest of $\frac{1}{2}$ a lime

3 tablespoons coconut flour

1 tablespoon coconut oil, plus extra for frying

5 eggs, beaten

sea salt and freshly ground black pepper, to taste

To serve

100 g (3$\frac{1}{2}$ oz) feta cheese (optional)

a small handful of coriander (cilantro) leaves

a small handful of basil leaves

1 tablespoon finely chopped dill

lemon wedges

125 ml (4 fl oz/$\frac{1}{2}$ cup) smoky tomato sauce (recipe opposite page)

Warm the oven to 150°C (300°F). Place 250 g (9 oz/1$\frac{3}{4}$ cups) of the peas and the rest of the pancake ingredients in a food processor and blitz to create a pea batter. Transfer to a bowl, then stir through the remaining peas.

Warm a large frying pan on a medium–low heat and melt $\frac{1}{2}$ a teaspoon of coconut oil at a time to cook the pancakes. I like to make small pancakes, which generally hold together best. To make these, drop 1 heaped tablespoon of the pea batter into the pan and press down lightly so the pancakes remain about 1– 1.5 cm ($\frac{1}{2}$–$\frac{5}{8}$ inch) thick.

Cook the pancakes for 3– 4 minutes on each side, or until golden, being careful not to flip them too soon on the first side as they may fall apart.

Once cooked, place on a platter, cover with foil and keep them warm in the oven while you cook the rest. Pack these up in a little container to carry to the beach and keep the sauce separate. Once you're there, simply sprinkle with feta (if using), herbs and a squeeze of lemon, then serve with some smoky tomato sauce and eat.

SERVES 4

Photograph page 99

The great thing about making your own condiments is that you can control exactly what goes into them and tweak the flavours until they are perfect for your specific tastes — meaning you get the experience of a gourmet sauce, but much cheaper! This sauce couldn't be easier to make: simmer for a few minutes then blitz. Easy! It is sensational with the pancakes opposite, in a bacon and egg roll, with barbecued chicken or beef ... anything you like, really.

Smoky tomato sauce

GF / DF / SF / V / VG

1 teaspoon coconut oil
½ a red onion, finely diced
400 g (14 oz) tomatoes, blanched, seeds removed, and diced, or 1 x 400 g (14 oz) tin of organic chopped tomatoes
1 teaspoon smoked paprika
sea salt and freshly ground black pepper
1 tablespoon maple syrup

In a small saucepan, melt the coconut oil over a low heat then add the onion and sauté for approximately 4 minutes. Add the tomatoes, smoked paprika and a good pinch of salt and pepper and simmer for 10 minutes, or until the sauce is slightly reduced.

Add the maple syrup and continue to cook for a further minute. Remove from the heat and allow to cool for a few minutes, then transfer to a food processor and blitz to create a smooth sauce. This can be served cold or warmed up a little.

Store in the fridge for up to 1 week.

MAKES 350 ML (12 FL OZ)

Photograph page 99

barbecue

Summer barbecues bring people together. Fact.

Overall, a barbecue menu can be really healthy and balance proteins, carbohydrates and fats from a variety of sources, which is one of the best things about this type of event. There are a few tricks that will make your barbecue really easy, tasty, nutritious *and* memorable. Here are a few things I've learned along the way.

Don't go crazy on the pre-barbecue snacks (chips, dips and the like). They take away from the main event and aren't necessary. It's best to let people build a little bit of hunger.

Avoid spending all your time standing over the heat of the coals. Prepare most things in advance and then cook just one or two items on the barbecue so you can actually spend time with your guests. Making protein-rich salads (using legumes, chicken or meat) are a great way to offer a little more in the menu without having to serve food that is hot off the fire.

Make your guests part of the culinary masterpiece. Most of the time the first question a guest will ask when invited is 'What can I bring?' If you don't feel like delegating salads or desserts, asking everyone to bring a piece of cheese for an epic platter at the end of the meal is a pretty sensational (and easy) thing to do.

SERVES 4

MAINS

RARE ROAST BEEF
WITH SLOW-ROASTED
BABY ROMA TOMATOES

BARBECUED WHITE
FISH WITH SUMMER
PAPAYA SALSA

SALADS

CHICKEN, MANGO
AND ALMOND SALAD

PESTO GREENS
AND QUINOA SALAD

CARROT SALAD

DESSERTS

ESPRESSO-CHOC
CHIA POPS

HUMMINGBIRD CAKE

Rare roast beef is incredibly tasty and it looks gourmet even though it's one of the simplest dishes to make. The secret is in the timing. To guarantee that gorgeous rare pink blush on thinly sliced beef, tie it with cooking string (not too tightly) before you get started to ensure an even thickness. Lightly sear it in a pan, then finish in a high oven for 20 minutes per kilo (2 lb 4 oz) of meat. The next vital step is to rest it for around 20–30 minutes so it is soft and delicious when sliced.

Rare roast beef with slow-roasted baby roma tomatoes

GF / DF / SF

1 kg (2 lb 4 oz) whole eye
    fillet of beef
300 g (10½ oz) baby roma
    tomatoes, halved
1 tablespoon olive oil
2 teaspoons balsamic
    vinegar
1 teaspoon grapeseed oil
sea salt and freshly ground
    black pepper
fresh herbs of choice
    for garnish (I like basil
    or parsley with this)

Take the beef out of the fridge about 30 minutes before cooking so it can come up to room temperature. Preheat the oven to 150°C (300°F) and line a baking tray (baking sheet) with baking paper.

Lay the roma tomatoes, cut side up, on the tray, drizzle with the olive oil and balsamic vinegar, then bake for 1½ hours. Remove from the oven and set aside. Increase the heat to 200°C (400°F) and prepare the beef.

Heat a large frying pan on a high heat and add the grapeseed oil. Season the beef well with salt and pepper, then tie with cooking string a few times, not too tightly

but securely enough to ensure the meat is a uniform thickness. Sear the beef briefly on all sides in the pan. This should only take a few minutes. Be careful not to burn or overcook the meat at this stage. Once the beef is browned, wrap it in foil and roast it in the oven for 20 minutes. Remove from the oven and allow to rest, still wrapped in foil, for a further 20–30 minutes.

To serve, finely slice the beef, then arrange on a platter with the warm slow-roasted tomatoes, a few sprigs of herbs to garnish and a pinch of salt and pepper.

SERVES 4-6

White fish has a lovely light flavour that works so well with a variety of accompaniments. For summer, I love serving it with the tropical flavours of the season: pineapple, papaya or mango. If you're preparing this as part of your barbecue menu, then cooking the fish while the beef rests is a really easy way to bring the timing of the mains together. This is also a great weeknight meal served with a simple salad.

Barbecued white fish with summer papaya salsa

GF / DF / SF

1.25 kg (2 lb 12 oz) barramundi or other white fish
sea salt and freshly ground black pepper
2 lemons
2 teaspoons olive oil

Papaya salsa
$\frac{1}{4}$ of a pineapple, diced
$\frac{1}{2}$ a papaya, diced
1 tablespoon lime juice
a handful of coriander (cilantro), leaves left whole, stalks finely chopped
1 teaspoon finely chopped bird's eye chilli, seeds removed

Heat your barbecue to 200°C (400°F). Lay out a large sheet of foil, place a sheet of baking paper on top of that and put the fish on top of this. Score it on both sides, to help it cook, then season with salt and pepper and drizzle over the juice of 1 lemon and the olive oil. Wrap the fish in the paper and foil to make an airtight parcel, then place on the barbecue to cook for 20 minutes on one side only.

While the fish is cooking, prepare the salsa by mixing all of the ingredients together in a serving bowl.

Once the fish is cooked (check this by gently pulling away the flesh closest to the bone, it should be opaque and flake easily), unwrap it and place on a serving platter. Cut the remaining lemon into wedges and serve with the fish and the bowl of salsa.

SERVES 4

I'll often put together yummy salads that are purely plant based, then team those with meat or fish to make a more substantial meal. But the summery sweet flavours of mango make this little number a nice change from the norm. I like incuding it as part of a larger meal, to diversify the salad offerings on the table, or simply having it on its own for lunch or a light dinner. The contrast between the sweetness of the mango and the savoury crunch of the almonds is a winning combo.

Chicken, mango and almond salad

GF / DF / SF

2 x 200 g (7 oz) chicken breasts, poached and sliced (see page 28 for method)
2 small mango cheeks, sliced
1 curly endive, leaves separated and torn
1 avocado, sliced
2 baby red radishes, finely sliced
140 g (5 oz) cherry tomatoes, halved
a small handful of dill
65 g ($2\frac{1}{4}$ oz/$\frac{1}{2}$ cup) slivered almonds, toasted

Dressing
3 tablespoons coconut cream
3 tablespoons extra virgin olive oil
$\frac{1}{2}$ a lemon
sea salt and freshly ground black pepper

On a large serving plate, arrange half of the chicken and half of the mango, endive, avocado, radish, cherry tomatoes, dill and almonds.

Combine all of the dressing ingredients and drizzle half over the salad. Top with the remaining salad ingredients to create a second layer then drizzle over the remaining dressing. Season well with salt and pepper and serve.

SERVES 4

This salad was one of the first really exciting taste sensations I ever created using quinoa. I think it has the best combination of texture, flavour and nutrition. Quinoa is such a versatile grain for both savoury and sweet, is gluten-free and has one of the highest amino acid profiles of all the grains.

Pesto greens and quinoa salad

GF / DF / SF / V / VG

200 g (7 oz/1 cup) quinoa, rinsed and drained

170 g (6 oz/1$\frac{1}{3}$ cups) fresh or frozen peas

100 g (3$\frac{1}{2}$ oz/1$\frac{2}{3}$ cup) broccoli florets

150 g (5$\frac{1}{2}$ oz/1 bunch) asparagus, woody ends trimmed, spears cut into thirds

2 tablespoons extra virgin olive oil

2 tablespoons kale and almond pesto (see recipe page 28)

2 tablespoons lemon juice

3 handfuls of rocket (arugula) leaves

2 silverbeet (Swiss chard) leaves, stalks discarded, leaves roughly torn

a handful of basil leaves

40 g (1$\frac{1}{2}$ oz/$\frac{1}{4}$ cup) pepitas (pumpkin seeds)

Celtic sea salt and freshly ground black pepper

Serve with 2 spring onions (scallions), green parts finely sliced (optional)

Put 375 ml (13 fl oz/1$\frac{1}{2}$ cups) of water and the quinoa in a small saucepan over a medium heat. Put the lid on and bring to the boil. Reduce the heat to a simmer, remove the lid and cook until the water is absorbed, the quinoa tails appear and the quinoa is tender — this should take about 15 minutes, but some quinoa grains can take up to 30 minutes.

While the quinoa cooks, blanch the peas, broccoli and asparagus so they are lightly cooked, but still have a little 'bite' to them. Plunge in iced water to refresh, then drain well and set aside.

Remove the saucepan from the heat and add the extra virgin olive oil, pesto and lemon juice, mixing in well so the quinoa becomes a lovely green colour. Set aside and allow to cool slightly.

In a large mixing bowl, combine the blanched peas, broccoli and asparagus with the rocket, silverbeet and basil leaves, and the pepitas. Add the warm quinoa and toss all the ingredients together gently. Season with salt and pepper, then either dish up or transfer to a serving dish before scattering over the spring onion, if using.

SERVES 4

Carrot salad

GF / DF / SF / V / VG

This salad brings a delightful, bright, summery vibe to the table, and is nutritious to boot. Carrots are rich in carotenoids — powerful antioxidants that support our eye health and protect against damage and ageing in our cells.

2 carrots, peeled into thin ribbons
55 g (2 oz/⅓ cup) almonds
55 g (2 oz/⅓ cup) sunflower seeds
a handful of coriander (cilantro),
  leaves picked, stalks finely chopped
a large handful of mint leaves
sea salt and freshly ground black pepper

Dressing
1 small garlic clove, crushed
a pinch of ground cinnamon
¼ teaspoon ground turmeric
½ teaspoon very finely diced ginger
1 tablespoon lemon juice
3 tablespoons extra virgin olive oil
1 teaspoon apple cider vinegar
1 teaspoon dijon mustard

Make the dressing by whisking all of the ingredients together in a small bowl.

Place all of the salad ingredients in a large serving bowl then drizzle over the dressing, toss lightly, season to taste and serve.

SERVES 4

Espresso-choc chia pops

GF / SF / V

This is a treat for all the big kids out there; a perfect blend of creamy natural Greek yoghurt, espresso coffee, raw chocolate and chia seeds, making for a dream combination of health and decadence. Chia seeds act as a great natural thickener for this 'ice cream', as the soluble fibre and omega-3 fats in the seeds create a gel-like substance that holds the ingredients together beautifully.

4 tablespoons coconut oil
60 g (2¼ oz/½ cup) raw cacao powder
1 tablespoon maple syrup

Frozen yoghurt
260 g (9¼ oz/1 cup) Greek-style yoghurt
3 tablespoons chia seeds
3 tablespoons maple syrup
3 tablespoons strong espresso coffee
½ teaspoon ground cinnamon

In a small saucepan, melt the coconut oil over a very low heat. Once melted, remove from the heat and whisk in the cacao powder and maple syrup.

In a large bowl whisk, together all of the ingredients for the frozen yoghurt until smooth.

Drop a teaspoon of your melted chocolate into each of the ice-cream moulds followed by the frozen-yoghurt mixture and finish with some more of the melted chocolate. Using a small spoon or ice-cream stick, give the popsicles a very light prod or stir so the chocolate oozes through the yoghurt a little as it freezes. Place your ice-cream sticks in each of the moulds and freeze overnight.

MAKES 4-6 MINI POPS

I love this cake because I created it for a girlfriend who adores anything cake-related, but especially the hummingbird cake. Hummingbird cake (which has nothing to do with humming or birds) is an insane mix of tropical sweetness. Traditional recipes call for tinned pineapple, which is typically high in refined sugars. But substituting fresh pineapple doesn't really pack quite enough pineapple punch, so my solution is to bake the fresh pineapple first, and this works a treat. Baked pineapple is also beautiful on top of Greek yoghurt with some crumbled macadamias, if you have any leftovers!

Hummingbird cake

GF / DF / SF / V

1 small pineapple, peeled and sliced into 1 cm ($\frac{1}{2}$ inch) rounds

1 teaspoon coconut oil, melted

Cake batter

100 g ($3\frac{1}{2}$ oz) unsalted butter, softened or 125 ml (4 fl oz/ $\frac{1}{2}$ cup) coconut oil, melted

3 tablespoons maple syrup

3 eggs, beaten

1 teaspoon ground cinnamon

1 teaspoon ground coriander

$\frac{1}{2}$ teaspoon ground cardamom

$\frac{1}{2}$ teaspoon bicarbonate of soda (baking soda)

2 teaspoons vanilla extract

a pinch of Celtic sea salt

2 ripe bananas, mashed

60 g ($2\frac{1}{4}$ oz/$\frac{2}{3}$ cup) coconut flour

50 g ($1\frac{3}{4}$ oz/$\frac{1}{2}$ cup) almond meal

35 g ($1\frac{1}{4}$ oz/$\frac{1}{2}$ cup) shredded coconut

Serve with a handful of chopped walnuts and Greek-style or coconut yoghurt

Preheat the oven to 180°C (350°F). Line a baking tray (baking sheet) with baking paper and put the pineapple slices on the tray. Drizzle over the coconut oil, toss to coat the slices, then spread them around the tray. Bake in the oven for 40 minutes. This should caramelise the pineapple beautifully and intensify its sweetness. Set the pineapple aside to cool.

Once the pineapple has cooled, roughly chop half of the rounds into bite-sized pieces, reserving the rest for later.

Line a 20 cm (8 inch) round cake tin with baking paper. In a large mixing bowl, beat the butter until light and creamy (if using coconut oil, do not whisk it, just add it to the other ingredients), then add the maple syrup, eggs, spices, bicarbonate of soda, vanilla and

salt. Add the mashed bananas and chopped pineapple pieces and mix everything together well.

Fold in the coconut flour, almond meal and shredded coconut. Lay half of the reserved pineapple rounds around the base of the tin, then pour half of the cake mixture over the top and jiggle it to spread it evenly. Add the remaining pineapple rounds, then pour over the rest of the batter and jiggle again. Bake in the oven for 45 minutes, or until golden on top and a skewer comes out clean. Allow the cake to cool in the tin for 20 minutes. Once cool, turn it out onto a rack to cool for a further 20 minutes.

Crumble the walnut pieces over the top and serve with yoghurt.

SERVES 8

cocktail party

Cocktail parties are some of the most challenging events to attend when you are focusing more attention on your health. I remember someone advising me to 'Stand next to the healthiest person at the cocktail party and eat as they do.' The reason being that you'll probably see them eating the lightest options and be encouraged to do the same by limiting the heavy pastries and fried foods, and alternating between water and any alcoholic drinks. That's the theory anyway!

By hosting your own cocktail party you have an opportunity to give every person in the room a chance to have a great time, in good health with good company. These are the experiences with food that really stand out for me. Avoid cooking foods that make people feel heavy or bloated, offer just a small selection of sweets and create a menu that appeals to the carni-, omni- and herbivores in the crowd.

About three-quarters of the way through the evening, unveil a grazing table with a big baked ham, an array of cheeses, some sliced sourdough baguettes, crackers, nuts, grapes and dates. If the party hasn't been vibing up to this point, this special touch will ensure it goes down in the history books.

SERVES 12

SAVOURY CANAPÉS

SHREDDED LEMON CHICKEN AND OREGANO TARTS

CHILLED AVO AND GREENS SOUP

RARE BEEF ON SEED SNAPS WITH PESTO

CARAMELISED ONION, ROSEMARY AND MANCHEGO FRITTATINA

TRUFFLED MUSHROOM PIZZETTAS

SUBSTANTIAL CANAPÉS

QUINOA MEATBALLS IN TOMATO SAUCE

LAMB RACKS WITH A CRANBERRY PLUM GLAZE

MOROCCAN FISH SKEWERS WITH HARISSA YOGHURT

SWEET CANAPÉS

SUMMER IN A POPSICLE

RAW DATE AND WALNUT BROWNIES

Pretty, substantial and full of flavour, these little tarts will make a grand entrance at any party, and they'll probably be snapped up before the serving tray makes it around the room. If you want to get ahead with your prep, make everything ahead of time and keep the filling in a bowl in the fridge, then assemble a few minutes before serving.

Shredded lemon chicken and oregano tarts

GF / DF / SF

Tart bases
70 g (2½ oz) besan
    (chickpea) flour
2–3 tablespoons
    coconut flour
½ teaspoon sea salt
2 tablespoons olive oil

Filling
400 g (14 oz) chicken
    breast, poached
    and shredded (see page 28
    for method)
2 tablespoons lemon juice
1 teaspoon finely grated
    lemon zest
4 tablespoons olive oil
1 tablespoon finely chopped
    flat-leaf (Italian) parsley
sea salt and freshly ground
    black pepper
1 small green apple,
    skin on, grated
2 tablespoons oregano
    leaves

Preheat the oven to 180°C (350°F) and arrange 24 miniature (2-tablespoon capacity) silicon moulds on a baking tray (baking sheet).

To make the tart bases, combine the besan flour with 2 tablespoons of the coconut flour and the salt in a food processor. Blitz briefly, then add the olive oil and 125 ml (4 fl oz/½ cup) of water and blitz once again to form a dough. Add the remaining tablespoon of coconut flour if the dough is too sticky.

Remove the dough from the food processor and roll out between two sheets of baking paper so it is about 5 mm (¼ inch) thick. Cut the dough with a cookie cutter approximately 7 cm (2¾ inches) in diameter, then press the rounds into the silicon moulds. Bake for 8-10 minutes in the oven, and then allow to cool before filling.

To make the tart filling, combine the chicken, lemon juice and zest, olive oil, parsley, salt and pepper in a bowl and toss to ensure an even distribution of flavours.

Place an equal amount of grated apple into each pastry case, top with the chicken mixture and finish with an oregano leaf on each tart.

MAKES 24 SMALL TARTS

SHREDDED LEMON CHICKEN
AND OREGANO TARTS

CHILLED AVO AND GREENS
SOUP *recipe page 118*

Chilled soup shots aren't served enough as far as I'm concerned — and boy should they be! You can easily prepare these in advance and serve them up in shot glasses or little teacups with a sprinkle of herbs on top. They bring great flair to a party and really amp up the plant-based nutrition on a canapé menu.

Chilled avo and greens soup

GF / DF / SF / V / VG

2 Lebanese cucumbers,
  chopped
2 large ripe avocadoes,
  destoned
2 zucchini (courgettes),
  chopped
2 small shallots (eschalots),
  chopped
2 large kale leaves, stalks
  removed, roughly torn
1 small fennel bulb,
  chopped, frondy tops
  reserved
4 tablespoons lemon juice
4 tablespoons flat-leaf
  (Italian) parsley leaves
4 tablespoons coriander
  (cilantro) leaves
1 teaspoon Celtic sea salt,
  or to taste
750 ml–1 litre
  (24 fl oz–35 fl oz/3–4 cups)
  filtered water

To garnish
finely chopped chives
  and fennel tops

Place all the ingredients, except the water, in a high-powered blender or food processor. Add 750 ml (26 fl oz/3 cups) of the water gradually and pulse until the mixture becomes a creamy soup. Adjust the texture to your liking, adding more or less water as needed. (You want to be able to drink this soup without feeling like you need a spoon to finish it.)

Taste and adjust the seasoning with any spices and additional herbs you like.

Pour into small serving glasses, shot glasses or espresso cups, garnish with finely chopped chives and fennel tops and serve.

SERVES 12, AS SMALL SHOTS

Photograph page 117

This is a great little combination of texture and flavour that uses many ingredients you might already have sitting in your fridge and pantry. The key to this canapé is the contrast in colours achieved when you cook the beef so it remains rare. Ensure you rest the beef properly so the meat softens and stays juicy; this will also make it easy to slice thinly and drape on top of the seed snap.

Rare beef on seed snaps with pesto

GF / DF / SF

400 g (14 oz) Scotch
   or eye fillet steak
grapeseed oil, for frying
24 seed snaps (see recipe
   on page 70)
4 tablespoons kale and
   almond pesto (see recipe
   on page 28)
sea salt and freshly ground
   black pepper
2 tablespoons freshly
   chopped herbs, such
   as chives, basil or
   parsley leaves

To cook the beef, heat a frying pan on a high heat and add a touch of grapeseed oil to coat the pan. Sear the steak for 3 minutes on each side, then set it aside and allow it to rest, uncovered, for 10 minutes. Once rested and cooled, finely slice the steak into 24 long pieces.

To create the canapés, place the seed snaps on a serving tray, evenly spread apart, then top each with ½ a teaspoon of pesto.

Follow with a thin slice of rare beef, delicately rolled to fit the seed snap so you get beautiful height in the presentation.

Finish with a good pinch of salt and pepper and garnish with the finely chopped herbs.

MAKES 24 CANAPÉS, 2 PER PERSON

Photograph page 121

Manchego cheese is something I came across by chance, but once I had a taste there was no looking back. It's a Spanish cheese made from sheep's milk, and it has a lovely gentle flavour. If you can't find Manchego, parmesan or goat's cheese will also taste beautiful in this frittatina. You can cook this in a loaf (bar) tin and layer the ingredients, or in smaller silicon moulds to create these delicious little morsels for the mouths of your guests.

Caramelised onion, rosemary and Manchego frittatina

GF / V

Caramelised onion

2 tablespoons grapeseed oil

1 large onion, finely sliced

2 tablespoons coconut sugar

2 tablespoons balsamic vinegar

Frittatina

12 eggs

sea salt and freshly ground black pepper

2 tablespoons finely chopped rosemary leaves

a small handful of rocket (arugula) leaves, finely chopped

100 g (3½ oz) Manchego cheese, crumbled

135 g (4¾ oz/½ cup) caramelised onion (see above)

First, make the caramelised onion. Put the grapeseed oil in a small frying pan over a medium heat. Add the onion and spread it evenly around the pan. Cook with the lid on for approximately 20 minutes, stirring occasionally, until softened and rich in colour. Reduce the heat to low and continue to cook for approximately 10 minutes more, stirring occasionally to prevent the onions sticking to the pan and burning.

Stir in the coconut sugar and balsamic vinegar and cook for a few minutes, or until the liquid has reduced, then remove from the heat. Once cool, the caramelised onion can be stored in a jar in the fridge for 4–5 days.

To make the frittatina, preheat the oven to 180°C (350°F) degrees and line a 14 × 24 cm (5½ × 9½ inch) loaf (bar) tin with baking paper.

Put the eggs in a mixing bowl and whisk. Season with salt and pepper and stir through the chopped rosemary and rocket leaves. Fold in the cheese. Pour the mixture into the lined loaf tin. Scatter over the caramelised onion, then bake on the top shelf of the oven for 45 minutes. Allow to cool for 20 minutes in the tin before removing and slicing into 24 pieces.

MAKES 24 SLICES, 2 PER PERSON

CARAMELISED
ONION, ROSEMARY
AND MANCHEGO
FRITTATINA

RARE BEEF ON SEED
SNAPS WITH PESTO
recipe page 119

People go crazy for these pizzettas every time I serve them at parties. They're a lovely alternative to wheat-based pizzas, and maintain the right balance of soft and crunch. Truffled mushrooms are delicious, but these bases go just as well with any topping you love: miso-glazed mushrooms, tomato and bocconcini with basil, roast pumpkin and feta ... the options are as endless as your imagination. As always with pizza, it's a matter of choosing your own adventure. If you go with this topping, the caramelised onion needs to be made ahead of time.

Truffled mushroom pizzettas

GF / DF / SF / V

Base

1 egg

1 tablespoon olive oil

50 g (1¾ oz/½ cup) almond meal

40 g (1½ oz/⅓ cup) coconut flour

½ teaspoon sea salt

Topping

2 tablespoons grapeseed oil or butter

200 g (7 oz) button mushrooms, brushed clean, quartered and finely sliced

1 tablespoon finely chopped flat-leaf (Italian) parsley leaves

2 tablespoons chervil leaves

150 g (5½ oz) enoki mushrooms

135 g (4¾ oz/½ cup) caramelised onion (see recipe on page 120)

sea salt and freshly ground black pepper

3–4 tablespoons truffle oil

To make the base, preheat the oven to 180°C (350°F) and line two baking trays (baking sheets) with baking paper.

Separate the egg yolk and white, putting the yolk in one medium mixing bowl and the white in another. Add the olive oil to the egg yolk and whisk together. Next, add the almond meal, coconut flour and salt. Stir well to combine. Once combined, add 1 tablespoon of warm water. The mixture should be slightly sticky at this point.

Whisk the egg white until white and fluffy, no peaks required, and fold this through the dough mixture. Place the dough between two sheets of baking paper and roll it out until it is approximately 5 mm (¼ inch) thick. Using a 4 cm (1½ inch) round cutter, cut the dough into circles and arrange them on the baking trays. Bake

in the oven for 12 minutes, then allow to cool on the trays for a few minutes before topping.

While the bases are cooking, make the topping. Warm a large saucepan on a medium heat and add half the grapeseed oil, followed by the button mushrooms and herbs, and sauté for 3–4 minutes. Add the enoki mushrooms for the final 1–2 minutes of cooking, then remove from the pan and set aside, covered with foil.

To finish the canapés, place a pinch of caramelised onion on each base, followed by the button mushrooms and a few enoki mushrooms. Finish with a good grinding of salt and pepper and a drizzle of truffle oil. Serve.

MAKES 24 PIZZETTAS, 2 PER PERSON

These meatballs first came about when I was developing gluten-free meal ideas for kids. My son, Jet, was young, and I wanted to reinvent the favourites I enjoyed growing up, but with better nutrition. Every time I made this dish, the adults would devour it just as eagerly as the children. Meatballs are generally a crowd pleaser, and with quinoa in place of breadcrumbs these little numbers are lighter and easier to digest than traditional meatballs and still absolutely scrumptious.

Quinoa meatballs in tomato sauce

GF / DF / SF

Quinoa meatballs

200 g (7 oz/1 cup) quinoa

375 g (13 oz) lean organic
  beef mince

3 tablespoons finely
  chopped flat-leaf (Italian)
  parsley leaves

2 tablespoon finely chopped
  basil leaves

2 small eggs, beaten

2 small garlic cloves,
  crushed

1 small onion, finely
  chopped

1½ teaspoons balsamic
  vinegar

1½ tablespoons tamari

3 tablespoons unsalted
  tomato paste

Tomato sauce

500 ml (9 fl oz/2 cups)
  tomato passata

2 garlic cloves, crushed

sea salt and freshly ground
  black pepper

Line a baking tray (baking sheet) with baking paper.

Rinse the quinoa under cold running water and place in a small saucepan with 500 ml (9 fl oz/ 2 cups) of water. Bring to the boil with the lid on, then reduce the heat, remove the lid and simmer until the water is absorbed. Fluff the quinoa up with a fork, then transfer to a large bowl. Add the remaining meatball ingredients and mix together really well. Shape into balls slightly smaller than a golf ball and pop onto the lined tray. Place in the fridge for at least 30 minutes to help the meatballs firm up.

Preheat the oven to 180°C (350°F) and bake the meatballs for 25–30 minutes.

While the meatballs are cooking, make the tomato sauce. Put the passata and garlic in a small saucepan and cook on a low heat for 15 minutes. Season with a good pinch of salt and pepper.

If you want to serve these on a platter, pour the sauce over the top and stick a toothpick in each meatball to make them easy for guests to pick up and eat.

**MAKES 24 MEATBALLS,
2 PER PERSON**

Roll these lamb racks out about three-quarters of the way through your party — they will be an absolute hit! Be sure to season the lamb well with salt and pepper before cooking, as the savoury, salty contrast with the cranberry plum glaze is what makes this item so delicious.

Lamb racks with a cranberry plum glaze

GF / DF / SF

300 g (10½ oz) plums
2 tablespoons cranberries (try to buy the ones sweetened with apple juice rather than coated with sugar)
3 tablespoons roughly chopped rosemary leaves
a pinch of ground cinnamon
grapeseed oil, for greasing
1.2 kg (2 lb 10 oz) lamb racks, fat trimmed, kept in racks of 4
sea salt and freshly ground black pepper

Place the plums, cranberries and 375 ml (13 fl oz/1½ cups) of water in a small saucepan on a medium heat. Cover and bring to the boil. Remove the lid, reduce the heat and simmer for 45 minutes.

Once reduced, cool slightly, then remove the plum skins and pits and briefly blitz the plums and cranberries with the rosemary leaves in a blender. Return to the pan, add the cinnamon and reduce for a further 15 minutes over a medium–low heat.

Preheat the oven to 220°C (425°F) and line a baking tray (baking sheet) with baking paper.

Heat a large frying pan on a high heat and lightly grease it with grapeseed oil. Season the lamb racks well with salt and pepper, then sear the meat for about 3 minutes on each side. Transfer to the oven to cook for a further 15–18 minutes (for medium–rare lamb). Remove from the oven and rest, covered with foil, for 10 minutes before slicing into individual servings.

Drizzle the cranberry plum glaze on the plate and between the portions of lamb, then serve.

SERVES 12

Moroccan food is a spectacular celebration of spices. Paprika, cinnamon, cumin, ginger and turmeric are all nourishing spices that support digestion and elimination. This spice combination is also a wonderful marinade for chicken skewers (try using a combination of breast and thigh). If you want to go that route, double the marinade and fry the chicken for 2–3 minutes in a pan to give it some nice colour before finishing it off in the oven.

Moroccan fish skewers with harissa yoghurt

GF / SF

1.2 kg (2 lb 10 oz) firm white
  skinless, boneless fish fillets
  (such as ling or hoki), cut
  into 2 cm (¾ inch) dice
grapeseed oil, for frying

Marinade
1 tablespoon sweet paprika
2 teaspoons ground cumin
1 teaspoon freshly
  grated ginger
2 teaspoons ground
  cinnamon
a good pinch of sea salt
1 teaspoon freshly
  grated turmeric
1 teaspoon apple cider vinegar
2 tablespoons grapeseed oil

Harissa yoghurt
260 g (9¼ oz/1 cup)
  Greek-style or natural
  full-fat yoghurt, or coconut
  cream if you want a
  non-dairy alternative,
½ teaspoon harissa paste

Serve with a small handful of
  coriander (cilantro) leaves
  and lemon wedges

Soak 24 wooden skewers (about 10 cm/4 inches long) in cold water; this prevents them burning during cooking. Line a baking tray (baking sheet) with baking paper.

Combine all of the ingredients for the marinade in a large bowl and stir well to combine. Using gloved hands or tongs, toss the fish pieces through the marinade until evenly coated. Thread the fish onto the skewers and place on the lined tray in the fridge to marinate for 30 minutes.

Combine the yoghurt and harissa in a small bowl and mix gently to combine. Put aside.

Heat a large frying pan or grill on a high heat and add a drizzle of grapeseed oil. Sear the fish skewers for about 4 minutes, turning often, so they are evenly cooked on all sides.

Serve with the harissa yoghurt, a small handful of coriander leaves sprinkled on top and a few lemon wedges for squeezing over.

MAKES 24 CANAPÉ-SIZED SKEWERS

Summer in a popsicle

GF / DF / SF / V / VG

Throughout the summer months there's a new popsicle flavour in our freezer every week. They're a simple combination of seasonal fruits and coconut milk, but if coconut milk isn't on hand it's completely fine to just use fruit. Make these popsicles even more beautiful by pushing fresh berries, slices of banana or mint into the moulds before freezing. To ensure they haven't melted by the time they reach the back of the room, present them to your guests on a serving platter covered with ice cubes — it works a treat.

600 ml (21 fl oz) coconut cream
2 bananas
1 mango, peeled and destoned
$1\frac{1}{2}$ tablespoons rice malt syrup
seeds from 1 vanilla bean or
$1\frac{1}{2}$ teaspoons vanilla extract

Put all of the ingredients in a blender and process until smooth and creamy. Divide between your popsicle moulds, add the popsicle sticks and freeze overnight.

For variety, consider adding:
• chopped raw chocolate, fresh or frozen raspberries or chopped macadamias in layers through the popsicle mould
• 2 tablespoons of peanut butter and 1 teaspoon of raw cacao powder before blending.

MAKES APPROXIMATELY 12 SMALL POPSICLES

Raw date and walnut brownies

GF / DF / SF / V

A lovely friend is responsible for introducing me to this delicious raw recipe. I'd just finished studying nutrition medicine but hadn't immersed myself in the raw treats culture yet; this was the turning point. This recipe is very simple and you can spruce it up with extra nuts, seeds or berries.

Brownie base
160 g ($5\frac{3}{4}$ oz) walnut halves
250 g (9 oz) Medjool dates, pitted
4 tablespoons raw cacao powder
  or unsweetened carob powder

Topping
4 tablespoons coconut oil, melted
1 tablespoon raw honey
1 tablespoon raw cacao powder
  or unsweetened carob powder

Serve with crushed walnuts sprinkled
  over the top (optional)

To make the base, blitz the walnuts to a fine crumb in a food processor. Add the dates and cacao powder or carob and process until slightly sticky and uniform in texture. Line a small square dish (I'll often just use a loaf/bar tin) with baking paper and press the mixture in firmly.

Place the coconut oil, honey and cacao in the food processor and process until you have a uniform texture. If the mixture is too thick, add a few drops of water. Spread evenly over the brownie in the tin using a spatula, then cover with plastic wrap and place in the fridge for 1 hour. This keeps for 2 weeks in the fridge or 4 in the freezer.

SERVES 12, 1 BITE EACH

DATE AND WALNUT
BROWNIES

SUMMER IN A POPSICLE

the family lunch

In the summer months my family does a lot of celebrating. We seize any and every opportunity to spend time together outside, ideally eating! I love the celebratory spirit of this season and am happiest when I'm organising gatherings that bring people together and showcase the beauty of food, nutrition and, of course, good company. Sometimes the events I plan are themed around a type of food (Italian, Mexican or Indian, for example); other times I just like to bring all of my favourite dishes into one space and let them create their own theme. Either way, I try to keep things as colourful as possible when it comes to the food (as a rule), and also balance different experiences within the meal so there is something for everyone.

SERVES 4

ENTRÉE

BEETROOT AND COCONUT CURED OCEAN TROUT

MAIN

SLOW-COOKED LAMB SHOULDER WITH CAPER JUS

SIDES

HEIRLOOM TOMATO SALAD

ASPARAGUS WITH DIJON-SPIKED YOGHURT

WARM PUMPKIN, QUINOA AND CABBAGE SALAD

DESSERTS

BANANA GELATO WITH GRILLED PINEAPPLE

CHIA AND LIME MACADAMIA TART

Cured fish makes a beautiful starter to share at a celebration. Surprisingly to many, it's actually incredibly easy to make, but it will require you to start preparing it one day in advance. You can use smaller fillets of fish, or buy one side of trout or salmon; just be sure to ask your fishmonger to remove the skin and pinbone the fish for you when you buy it.

Beetroot and coconut cured ocean trout

GF / DF

150 g (5½ oz) beetroot
   (beets), peeled and grated
120 g (4¼ oz/¾ cup)
   coconut sugar
50 g (1¾ oz) rock salt
2 tablespoons finely
   chopped dill
1 teaspoon finely grated
   lime zest
350 g (12 oz) ocean trout
   (see intro), skinned
   and pinboned
1 spelt (or gluten-free)
   baguette
2 tablespoons olive oil
sea salt

Serve with quark or crème
   fraîche, and caviar if it's a
   really special occasion
   (optional), microherbs
   and lemon wedges

The day before you want to serve this, combine the grated beetroot with the coconut sugar, rock salt, dill and lime zest in a small bowl to make a curing mix. Spread half of this mix in a glass dish (that the fish can sit in snugly) and place the trout on top. Rub the remaining curing mixture all over the flesh, ensuring the fish is completely covered. Cover the dish with plastic wrap, then leave in the fridge overnight to cure.

The next day, remove the fish from the dish and wipe it down with a paper towel, ensuring all of the curing mixture is cleaned off. Using a very sharp knife, slice the fish into thin pieces.

To make crostata to serve with the fish, preheat the oven grill (broiler) to medium–high. Thinly slice the baguette on the diagonal and arrange on a baking tray (baking sheet). Drizzle with olive oil and sprinkle with salt. Grill (broil) for 2–3 minutes on each side, or until lightly golden. Allow to cool slightly.

To serve, arrange the crostata on a serving platter. Top with slices of the fish, little spoonfuls of quark or crème fraîche (and caviar, if you like), a pinch of fresh microherbs and lemon wedges.

SERVES 4

Shoulder is one of the most flavoursome cuts from the lamb, so it doesn't need marinades or too much else for you to experience a delicious explosion of taste in your first mouthful. I've made a very simple caper and mint jus to accompany this, as the saltiness of capers with the lamb falling off the bone is one of the best marriages in food ever. This lamb is sensational served with the olive and broccoli tapenade on page 74, too.

Slow-cooked lamb shoulder with caper jus

GF / DF / SF

1 lamb shoulder, bone in
  (approximately 1.8–2 kg/
  4 lb–4 lb 8 oz)
sea salt
1 tablespoon grapeseed oil,
  plus extra for drizzling
1 garlic bulb, halved
  horizontally
a good handful of rosemary
  sprigs, plus extra to serve
freshly ground black
  pepper

Caper jus
250 ml (9 fl oz/1 cup)
  chicken or vegetable stock
2 tablespoons capers
a large handful of mint
  leaves, finely sliced, plus
  a few whole leaves
  to serve
2 teaspoons cornflour
  (cornstarch) or
  brown rice flour

Preheat the oven to 150°C (300°F). Lightly score the skin of the lamb on the diagonal and season with a teaspoon of salt and a drizzle of grapeseed oil. Place a flameproof casserole dish on a medium–low heat on the stove and add the tablespoon of oil. Sear the lamb shoulder for 5 minutes, ensuring all sides are evenly browned.

Remove the dish from the heat and tuck the garlic halves and the rosemary underneath the lamb. Season with pepper then pour the stock around the lamb. Cover with a lid or two layers of foil, sealed at the edge of the dish, and cook in the oven for 4–5 hours. Check after 4 hours to see how tender and melty the lamb is; if it needs longer, continue cooking. The longer the meat cooks, the yummier it should be.

Once cooked, set the lamb aside, covered with foil, and make the caper jus. Pour the stock from the casserole dish into a small saucepan over a medium heat and squeeze in the garlic purée from the cooked bulbs. Add the capers and mint and bring to the boil.

Pour 4 tablespoons of the jus into a small jug and whisk in the cornflour until a smooth paste is formed. Return this paste to the saucepan and whisk in well. Reduce to a simmer and cook for a further 5 minutes to ensure the cornflour is dissolved and cooked.

To serve, place the lamb shoulder on a platter and garnish with some fresh mint leaves and rosemary sprigs. Stab a serving knife and fork into the top of the lamb so you can pull the deliciously melting meat apart at the table. Serve a little bowl or jug of jus on the side.

SERVES 4

Heirloom tomato salad

GF / DF/ SF / V / VG

Brightly coloured heirloom tomatoes are robust and have a brilliant flavour that should be celebrated with other ingredients of the same nature: fresh basil leaves, sea salt, apple cider vinegar and the best extra virgin olive oil you can get your hands on. This is all you need to turn a very simple salad into something really special.

600 g (1 lb 5 oz) mixed heirloom tomatoes,
  sliced or quartered
a large handful of basil leaves
1 tablespoon good-quality extra virgin olive oil
1½ tablespoons apple cider vinegar
sea salt and freshly ground black pepper

Arrange the tomatoes and basil leaves on a serving plate or in a shallow bowl. Drizzle with the olive oil and apple cider vinegar, season with salt and pepper and serve.

SERVES 4

Asparagus with dijon-spiked yoghurt

GF / SF / V

By now you may have realised that I am a fan of Greek and natural yoghurts. I love them because good-quality, organic, full-cream yoghurt is rich in calcium, protein and probiotic strains, which are beneficial for the growth of healthy gut bacteria. Yoghurt is often well-tolerated by those who have issues with dairy milk because it contains significantly less lactose. It's great in dressings, adding creaminess to soups or for serving with baked eggs or frittatas.

½ teaspoon coconut or grapeseed oil
150 g (5½ oz/ 1 bunch) asparagus,
  woody ends trimmed
95 g (3¼ oz/⅓ cup) natural yoghurt
1 teaspoon dijon mustard
sea salt and freshly ground black pepper
40 g (1½ oz/¼ cup) toasted hazelnuts or almonds,
  roughly chopped
a small handful of chervil leaves, or other
  soft herbs of your choice

Heat a large frying pan or cast-iron grill on a high heat and add the oil. Add the asparagus spears and cook for 5 minutes, tossing occasionally to ensure an even colour.

While the asparagus is cooking, combine the yoghurt, mustard and a pinch of salt.

Arrange the asparagus on a serving plate and drizzle over the spiked yoghurt. Top with the nuts and herbs and serve with a good grinding of black pepper.

SERVES 4

HEIRLOOM
TOMATO SALAD

Warm pumpkin, quinoa and cabbage salad

GF / DF / SF / V / VG

750 g (1 lb 10 oz) pumpkin (winter squash),
  skin on, seeds removed, sliced into 8 pieces
1 tablespoon grapeseed oil
a good pinch of sea salt
140 g (5 oz) cooked red quinoa
a small handful of flat-leaf (Italian) parsley leaves
130 g (4¾ oz) red cabbage, finely shredded
60 g (2¼ oz/½ cup) walnuts, toasted

Dressing
2 tablespoons extra virgin olive oil
1 teaspoon balsamic vinegar
a pinch of ground cinnamon
1 teaspoon maple syrup (optional)

Preheat the oven to 200°C (400°F) and line a large baking tray (baking sheet) with baking paper.

Toss the pumpkin slices in the oil and salt and arrange on the tray so they lay as flat as possible; this helps keep them whole for presentation. Bake in the oven for 20 minutes, or until golden.

Once cooked, arrange the pumpkin in layers on a large serving platter with the quinoa, parsley, cabbage and walnuts.

Combine all of the dressing ingredients together, then drizzle over the salad. Serve while warm (although this salad is also delicious served cold).

SERVES 4

Banana gelato with grilled pineapple

GF / DF / SF / V / VG

If you don't have, or don't want to use, coconut cream in this recipe, frozen bananas on their own will also work well. The coconut cream just gives it a little more of that tropical summer vibe and adds a great creaminess, similar to ice cream.

150 g (5½ oz) pineapple, peeled and sliced into
  1 cm (½ inch) thick semi-circles (no need
  to remove the core)
4 large frozen bananas
60 g (2¼ oz/¼ cup) coconut cream
1 teaspoon vanilla extract or vanilla paste

Preheat the oven grill (broiler) to high and line a baking tray (baking sheet) with baking paper.

Arrange the pineapple pieces evenly on the tray and grill (broil) for 6 minutes on each side, until they are lightly golden and starting to become crispy around the edges. Allow the pineapple to cool then slice each piece in half.

While the pineapple is grilling, place the frozen bananas, coconut cream and vanilla in a high-powered blender and blitz until a beautiful creamy consistency is created.

To serve, scoop generous spoonfuls of the banana gelato into glasses or bowls and top with the pineapple pieces.

SERVES 4

WARM PUMPKIN, QUINOA
AND CABBAGE SALAD

This tart is a special one in my health journey, career and life, and it's absolutely a recipe worth sharing. It is a beautiful and creamy dairy-free alternative to cheesecake that also happens to be devoid of gluten and refined sugars, which to me is a dessert delight. Created by my lovely friend Fiona, it will nourish and energise you and your guests.

Chia and lime macadamia tart

GF / DF / V / VG

Tart base
3 tablespoons melted coconut oil, plus extra for greasing
190 g (6¾ oz/1½ cups) macadamia nuts
1 tablespoon macadamia nut butter
1 tablespoon coconut sugar
45 g (1¾ oz/½ cup) desiccated coconut
finely grated zest of 1 lime

Filling
220 g (7¾ oz/1½ cups) raw cashews, soaked for 8 hours
80 g (2¾ oz/½ cup) coconut sugar
185 ml (6 fl oz/¾ cup) lime juice (about 4–5 limes)
400 ml (14 fl oz) coconut cream
1 teaspoon vanilla extract
60 g (2¼ oz/⅓ cup) chia seeds

Garnish with finely grated lime zest

Line or grease a 20 cm (8 inch) springform tin with a little coconut oil. To make the tart base, put the macadamias in a food processor and whiz to a fine crumb. Add the macadamia butter, coconut sugar, desiccated coconut, 3 tablespoons of coconut oil and lime zest and whiz again to combine. Press this mixture evenly into the base and side of the tin, then put in the freezer for 30 minutes.

To make the filling, rinse and drain the soaked cashews, then place them in a food processor with the coconut sugar and lime juice.

Combine until the sugar is well blended. Pour in the coconut cream and vanilla and blitz again until creamy. Stir through the chia seeds. Pour the filling into the base, spread around evenly, then cover with plastic wrap and place in the freezer overnight, or for at least 8 hours, until set.

Remove from the freezer and allow to soften for 10 minutes before serving. You can store this in the fridge for up to 1 week, or in the freezer for up to 2 weeks.

SERVES 8

autumn

Autumn is a magical time of change, colour and nourishment. I see more people slowing down with the cool change during this transition between the seasons than at any other time. They reduce commitments, spend more time indoors and become a little less active. And as we slow down, so should the way we eat. Autumn is a time to ready ourselves for the winter with foods that moisten the body and support the immune system before the cold and dryness of winter is upon us. Powerful flavours such as garlic, ginger, horseradish, lemon and chilli, as well as ingredients such as leek, sweet potato, mushroom, spinach, nuts and seeds are perfect to integrate into your autumn menus.

Draw on the colours of this season when presenting your meals by weaving them into your decorative touches. Deep oranges, golden yellows or rich reds splashed through the table settings in the form of stems of berries, fallen leaves or linens are beautiful and nod to many of the foods you are serving.

AUTUMN VEGETABLES

ASIAN GREENS
BEANS
BEETROOT (BEETS)
BROCCOLI
BRUSSELS SPROUTS
CABBAGE
CAPSICUM (PEPPER)
CARROT
CELERY
CHILLI
CUCUMBER
DAIKON
FENNEL
GARLIC
GINGER
GREEN BEANS
HORSERADISH
LEEK
LETTUCE
MUSHROOMS
OKRA
OLIVES
ONION
PARSNIP
POTATO
SILVERBEET
  (SWISS CHARD)
SHALLOT
SPINACH
SWEET POTATO
TOMATO
ZUCCHINI (COURGETTE)

AUTUMN FRUITS

APPLE
AVOCADO
BANANA
CUMQUAT
CUSTARD APPLE
FIG
KIWI FRUIT
LEMON
LIME
MANDARIN
NECTARINE
ORANGE
PAPAYA
PEAR
PLUM
POMEGRANATE
QUINCE

the dinner party

Admittedly, I hadn't cooked that many multi-course meals until I started the catering arm of my business, and then I was really put to the challenge. Planning this type of sit-down meal is fun (seriously, I mean that) but it does force you to get your head around being really organised, toning things back a little and showing a delicate hand in the kitchen in order to bring these smaller dishes to life and make them part of a bigger story.

What I've created on the following pages is a seven-course menu that showcases lots of beautiful seasonal flavours. As you read it, you'll begin to realise that you'll need a few different serving dishes for your guests. But don't worry, this doesn't mean investing in a new dinnerware set. My tip is to get creative. Use small teacups for the soup, side plates for the fish, small saucers for the salad, dinner plates for the meat, shot glasses for the granita and entrée plates for the crêpes. Hopefully you'll have many of these on hand already; if not, you can easily pick them up at vintage, thrift or knick-knack stores for next to nothing. Serving this way makes the table really fun, and that's what a party should be.

SERVES 4

ENTRÉE 1

TRUFFLED CELERIAC
SOUP WITH CROSTATA

ENTRÉE 2

KINGFISH CEVICHE
WITH LEMON, GINGER
AND CUCUMBER

MAIN COURSE

SCOTCH FILLET
WITH EGGPLANT PURÉE
AND MISO BUTTER

SALAD

FENNEL, RADISH, APPLE
AND CELERY SALAD

REFRESHER

MANDARIN CAMU
GRANITA

DESSERT

CACAO BESAN CRÊPES
WITH RAW CASHEW AND
COCONUT ICE CREAM

NIGHT BITE

RAW CACAO TRUFFLES

FENNEL, RADISH, APPLE AND CELERY SALAD *recipe page 152*

Truffles are a type of funghi, and black truffles, which grow near oak and hazelnut trees, are a true culinary delicacy. They can be hard to source and very expensive but they do share their deep flavour and a touch of decadence with just about anything they are added to. Truffle oil, which is extra virgin olive oil infused with truffle, is a less expensive way to include that special flavour in your cooking. It complements the celeriac and the creaminess of potato exquisitely, but is quite a powerful ingredient, so be careful not to drizzle too much over the soup.

Truffled celeriac soup with crostata

GF OPTION / DF / SF / V / VG

2 tablespoons grapeseed oil
1 small onion, roughly
    chopped
500 g (1 lb 2 oz) celeriac,
    peeled and roughly
    chopped
200 g (7 oz) potatoes, peeled
    and roughly chopped
700 ml (24 fl oz) vegetable
    stock (you can use chicken
    stock, if you aren't
    vegetarian or vegan)
1 teaspoon nutritional
    yeast
sea salt and freshly ground
    black pepper
2–3 tablespoons truffle oil,
    to taste
finely chopped herbs of your
    choice to finish (chives,
    thyme and oregano are
    my favourites)
toasted spelt (or gluten-free)
    baguette, to serve

Heat the grapeseed oil in a medium-sized saucepan on a low heat. Add the onion and sauté for 5 minutes, or until translucent and soft. Add the celeriac, potato and stock, bring to the boil, then turn down to a simmer and cook for 40 minutes, or until the vegetables are tender. Add the nutritional yeast as it finishes cooking, then

allow to cool slightly before puréeing in a high-speed blender.

Season with salt and pepper, then divide between serving bowls. Drizzle a little truffle oil over the soup and garnish with the herbs and another grind of pepper. Serve with slices of the toasted baguette.

SERVES 4

Ceviche is an incredibly quick and easy dish to pull together and the flavours are fresh and clean. The kingfish picks up on the citrus and herbs beautifully and contrasts perfectly with the crunch of the cucumber and celery. It literally takes minutes to put together after the initial prep, and is made to impress. I'll often whip this dish up for a light lunch, too — it's very versatile.

Kingfish ceviche with lemon, ginger and cucumber

GF / DF / SF

250 g (9 oz) piece of
   sashimi-grade kingfish,
   skin and bones removed,
   sliced into 1 cm ($\frac{1}{2}$ inch)
   thick pieces
juice of 1 lemon (at least
   3 tablespoons)
juice of 1 lime (at least
   2 tablespoons)
1 teaspoon freshly
   grated ginger
$\frac{1}{4}$ of a red onion,
   finely chopped
2 celery stalks, finely sliced
   or shaved
1 telegraph cucumber,
   finely sliced or shaved
a small handful of
   mint leaves, shredded
a small handful of
   coriander (cilantro) leaves

Combine the kingfish pieces, citrus juices and ginger in a bowl and set aside to marinate for approximately 3–4 minutes.

Drain the excess marinade from the kingfish, then toss the fish with the onion, celery, cucumber, mint and coriander, then serve straight away.

SERVES 4

Creamy miso butter and really good-quality grass-fed, free-range meat are the key components of this dish. Both create an absolutely melt-in-your-mouth sensation that is incomparable; this is probably one of my favourite ways to eat red meat. Miso butter can also be used to melt over a piece of grilled salmon or trout, spread on toast then topped with grilled mushrooms, or to fry scrambled eggs.

Scotch fillet with eggplant purée and miso butter

GF / DF / SF

1 x 400 g (14 oz) piece
 of Scotch fillet
2 large eggplants
 (aubergines)
1 tablespoon grapeseed oil
sea salt and freshly ground
 black pepper
a small handful of baby
 spinach leaves
100 g (3½ oz) miso butter,
 softened (see below)
1 tablespoon finely chopped
 chives or microherbs,
 to garnish

Miso butter
100 g (3½ oz) butter,
 softened
1½ tablespoons white
 miso paste

Preheat the oven to 200°C (400°F) and line a baking tray (baking sheet) with baking paper. Take the meat out of the fridge so it has time to come to room temperature before cooking.

Slice the eggplants down the middle, keeping their top ends connected so you can join their halves back together. Rub a little grapeseed oil on the flesh, and then push the two halves back together; this will create a steaming effect during cooking. Put the eggplants on the baking tray and bake in the oven for 15 minutes.

While the eggplants are cooking, make the miso butter. Combine the softened butter and miso paste in the small bowl of a food processor or use a hand beater and beat until light and fluffy, then set aside.

When the eggplant is cooked, remove it from the oven and allow to cool for a few minutes before handling. Separate the halves, scoop out the flesh and place it in a blender with a good pinch of salt and pepper. Blitz briefly to create a purée.

Season the meat well with salt and pepper. Heat an ovenproof frying pan on a high heat and drop a touch of oil into the pan, followed by the meat. Sear for 2 minutes on each side, then place in the oven to cook for a further 5 minutes. Remove from the oven, cover with foil and allow to rest for 5 minutes.

Prepare the plates while the meat is resting. If you want to cook the spinach, fry it gently in a pan over a medium heat with a drizzle of oil until just wilted. Evenly portion the eggplant purée on each plate, followed by a few leaves of raw or wilted baby spinach. Thinly slice the meat across the grain and create a fan of the pieces on top of the eggplant purée. Finish with a spoonful of miso butter to melt over each serving of meat and a sprinkle of herbs to garnish.

SERVES 4

Fennel, radish, apple and celery salad

GF / DF / SF / V / VG

I've included this refreshing salad because it combines some of my absolute favourites in crunchy salad flavours. Incidentally, it also pairs beautifully with grilled salmon or the slow-roasted pork on page 238.

1 small fennel bulb, finely sliced
2 rainbow or red radishes, trimmed
  and finely sliced
2 celery stalks, finely sliced into matchsticks
1 small red apple, finely sliced into matchsticks
1 tablespoon lemon juice
walnut oil, to drizzle
2 tablespoons chervil leaves
sea salt and freshly ground black pepper

Combine the fennel, radish, celery, apple and lemon juice in a bowl and toss to combine.

Divide equally between four serving plates. Drizzle over a little walnut oil, sprinkle over the chervil leaves and finish with a good pinch of salt and pepper.

SERVES 4

Photograph page 144

Mandarin camu granita

GF / DF / SF / V

Granita works as a refreshing palate cleanser in between dishes. If mandarins aren't available, then oranges or a combination of lemon, lime and orange are good substitutes. Camu has a yummy citrus taste, and will up the antioxidant factor in the granita, too.

250 ml (9 fl oz/1 cup) freshly squeezed
  mandarin juice
1 tablespoon raw honey
1 tablespoon camu powder

Blend all of the ingredients together then pour into a freezer-friendly container. Place in the freezer for 6–8 hours, or overnight, if you want to be organised.

Bring out of the freezer 5 minutes before serving to allow the granita to soften slightly. Use a fork to scrape into shards, then divide between your shot glasses or small cups and serve — quickly, before it melts!

SERVES 4 (AS A TASTER BETWEEN COURSES)

MANDARIN CAMU GRANITA

Crêpes are a lovely light way to finish a meal. These besan flour versions are generally easier to digest than wheat-based crêpes. You'll see I've written that this makes four to six, even though this menu is only for four people. That's because, for some reason, the first crêpe is usually a test and never turns out that well! Allow yourself to find your crêpe-making groove and then produce the remainder, ready to serve up with ice cream.

Cacao besan crêpes

GF / DF / SF / V / VG

120 g ($4\frac{1}{4}$ oz/1 cup) besan
   (chickpea) flour
1 tablespoon raw
   cacao powder
$\frac{1}{4}$ teaspoon ground ginger
$\frac{1}{4}$ teaspoon sea salt
$\frac{1}{2}$ teaspoon ground cinnamon
2 teaspoons bicarbonate
   of soda (baking soda)
1 teaspoon vanilla extract
3 tablespoons maple syrup
coconut oil, for frying
a few mint leaves,
   to serve (optional)

Serve with sliced kiwi,
   passionfruit, berries or
   other nice seasonal fruit.
   If you want to really go for
   it, you could also serve with
   a scoop of cashew and
   coconut ice cream (see page
   156) or Greek-style, vanilla
   or natural yoghurt.

Sift the besan flour and cacao into a mixing bowl. Stir through the ginger, salt and cinnamon.

In a jug, whisk together 300 ml ($10\frac{1}{2}$ fl oz) of water and the bicarbonate of soda until it has completely dissolved. Add the vanilla extract and maple syrup, stirring well to combine.

Slowly whisk the wet ingredients into the dry mixture until light and fluffy. Cover the batter with plastic wrap and place in the refrigerator for 30 minutes.

Preheat the oven to a very low temperature and heat a large frying pan over a medium heat. Add a little coconut oil to the pan. Pour 3 tablespoons of batter into the pan and swirl the mixture around the pan to create a thin crêpe. Allow the crêpe to cook until the edges start to slightly brown and the surface is bubbly, then flip it over with a flat spatula. Cook on the other side for around 30 seconds. Transfer to a plate, cover with foil and pop in the oven to keep warm, then repeat this process with the remaining crêpe batter.

Top each crêpe with a scoop of raw cashew and coconut ice cream (if using), some fresh fruit and mint leaves (if using), then serve.

MAKES 4–6 CRÊPES

CACAO BESAN CRÊPES

RAW CASHEW AND
COCONUT ICE CREAM
recipe page 156

This is a raw ice cream, which means none of the ingredients have been treated by heat and therefore they retain more of their nutritional value. It is also dairy-free, so it's a fabulous alternative to regular ice cream. Cashews are rich in oleic acid, which is a monounsaturated oil said to protect against cardiovascular disease and cancer. When cashews are soaked before being blitzed, it adds an insane creaminess to raw treats that you don't get from other nuts without the flavour of the nut overpowering the rest of the experience.

Raw cashew and coconut ice cream

GF / DF / SF / V / VG

80 g (2¾ oz/½ cup) raw cashews, soaked in water overnight

135 g (4¾ oz/½ cup) unhulled tahini

250 g (9 oz/1 cup) coconut flesh (approximately 1 fresh coconut)

125 ml (4 fl oz/½ cup) coconut milk or coconut cream

4 tablespoons maple syrup (see note below)

1 tablespoon vanilla paste or seeds from 1 vanilla bean

2 tablespoons coconut oil

Note: you can reduce the amount of maple syrup or use 125 ml (4 fl oz/ ½ cup) rice malt syrup in its place for a fructose-free alternative

Combine all of the ingredients except the coconut oil in a high-speed blender or food processor and blitz until creamy. Add the coconut oil and blitz again. Pour into a large container and freeze for at least 6 hours, or until set.

Prior to serving, blitz again to a lovely gelato consistency, then serve right away.

SERVES 4–6

Photograph page 155

The base truffle recipe here is delicious all by itself, but for something a little fancier, I like to mix things up a little. Try my flavour variations below. Choose your favourites, then work those into the base mixture. But please keep in mind that the quantities of the optional flavours are intended for a third of the mixture. Scale up if you want to use a particular flavour for all of the truffles.

Raw cacao truffles

GF / DF / SF / V / VG

100 g (3½ oz) coconut flesh (approximately ½ a fresh coconut)

55 g (2 oz/⅓ cup) almonds

50 g (1¾ oz/⅓ cup) cashews

40 g (1½ oz/¼ cup) pepitas (pumpkin seeds)

4 tablespoons raw cacao powder

85 g (3 oz/½ cup) Medjool dates, pitted

80 g (2¾ oz/½ cup) dried apricots

125 ml (4 fl oz/½ cup) coconut cream

Combine all of the ingredients in a food processor and blitz until well combined. Divide the mixture into three portions and add your choice of different flavourings from the options below before rolling into small truffles.

Alternatively, you can roll teaspoons of this base mixture into balls, then roll them in desiccated coconut until completely coated.

Store in an airtight container for up to 2 weeks in the fridge or 1 month in the freezer.

MAKES 36 TRUFFLES

Cherry acai (for 12 balls)

30 g (1 oz/¼ cup) dried cherries

2 tablespoons acai powder

Place 2 dried cherries in the centre of a heaped teaspoon of the base mixture. Roll into balls between your palms then into the acai powder to coat. Place on a lined baking tray (baking sheet) and refrigerate.

Almond (for 12 balls)

12 almonds

25 g (1 oz/¼ cup) almond meal

Place one almond in the centre of a heaped teaspoon of the base mixture. Roll into balls between your palms and then into the almond meal to coat. Place on a lined baking tray (baking sheet) and refrigerate.

Mint (for 12 balls)

3 drops of mint essence

2 teaspoons raw cacao powder

Blend the mint essence into the base mixture. Roll heaped teaspoons of the mixture into balls between your palms and then into the raw cacao to coat. Place on a lined baking tray (baking sheet) and refrigerate.

a warming brunch

As the months of autumn progress, the mornings become darker and by the time the weekend rolls around our bodies crave a little more rest in the early hours. Indulge that with a later start and make brunch an occasion to bring together the best hours of the morning and early afternoon, celebrated with a more substantial menu. I like to keep my brunches more on the savoury side, and introduce sweetness via seasonal fruits in smoothies and tea.

Whenever I'm creating an autumn brunch for clients (or my wonderful friends), I like to decorate the table with a few beautiful autumn leaves, use simple material placemats in rustic and neutral tones, and set jugs and jars of seasonal branches and flowers around the environment to bring warmth and life to the room.

SERVES 4

TO DRINK

BEETROOT, CARROT AND ORANGE SMOOTHIE

KI-LIME SMOOTHIE

CINNAMON, CARDAMOM AND ORANGE TEA

SALTED CARAMEL SMOOTHIE WITH BEE POLLEN

TO EAT

SMOKED SALMON AND BABY BRUSSELS

BAKED EGGS WITH SPINACH AND LABNEH

SAUTÉED KALE WITH BUTTERBEANS, GARLIC AND PARMESAN

GRILLED MUSHROOMS WITH TAHINI AND CHILLI

PUMPKIN, CARROT AND HERB LOAF

Beetroot, carrot and orange smoothie

GF / DF / SF / V / VG

The beautiful deep fuchsia hues of this smoothie reflect the changing colours of autumn. They also bring life to the table and, of course, your body. This great vegetable-based smoothie is sweet enough just from the beetroot, carrots and orange. Be sure to blend the mixture really well as the fibre in the beetroot and carrot will naturally make it thicker than other blends.

1 small beetroot (beet), peeled and quartered
2 small carrots, roughly chopped
500 ml (17 fl oz/2 cups) coconut water, chilled
a small handful of fresh mint leaves
½ an orange, peeled and halved

Combine all of the ingredients in a blender and blitz until smooth. Pour into glasses and set out on the table with the ki-lime smoothie so people can help themselves and have a taste of each smoothie as they please.

MAKES 4 SMALL GLASSES

Ki-lime smoothie

GF / DF / SF / V / VG

One of my favourite green blends, this smoothie has a delicious zesty flavour from kiwi, lime and coriander. The sour and bitter flavours of lime are great for stimulating the liver and also complement the kiwi, which contains a wicked burst of digestive enzymes that help break down and absorb the nutrition in your food.

500 ml (17 fl oz/2 cups) coconut water, chilled
1 kiwi fruit, peeled
1 pear, cored and roughly chopped
1 cucumber, halved
20 g (¾ oz/¼ of a bunch) coriander (cilantro),
  including stalks (roots removed)
½ a zucchini (courgette)
1 lime, peeled and white pith removed
2 teaspoons camu powder
a pinch of ground cinnamon

Combine all of the ingredients in a blender and blitz until smooth. Put out on the table with the beetroot and orange smoothie so people can help themselves.

MAKES 4 SMALL GLASSES

KI-LIME SMOOTHIE

BEETROOT, CARROT AND
ORANGE SMOOTHIE

Smoked salmon and baby brussels

GF / DF / SF

Smoked salmon is a staple at any brunch I prepare, either for friends or family. It brings more protein to the table, feels a touch decadent and works wonders when cooked with these humble sprouts.
In my experience, brussels sprouts need a salty ingredient to bring out their delicious flavour, so smoked salmon complements them really well, as does bacon, capers or parmesan.

180 g (6 oz) smoked salmon
1 teaspoon grapeseed oil
300 g (10½ oz) baby brussels sprouts, trimmed and halved
½ teaspoon finely grated lemon zest
2 tablespoons finely chopped dill
a small handful of flat-leaf (Italian) parsley leaves
½ a lemon, to serve

Slice the salmon into long strips about 2 cm (¾ inch) wide. Warm a large frying pan on a medium heat then add the oil. Add the brussels sprouts to the pan and cook for 3 minutes, moving them all around the pan. Toss the salmon strips through the sprouts, add the lemon zest and cook a further 2 minutes.

Remove from the pan, sprinkle over the herbs, give everything a good squeeze of lemon and serve.

SERVES 4

Baked eggs with spinach and labneh

GF / SF / V

Baked eggs were introduced to me by one of my gorgeous friends and I have never looked back. My top tip when cooking this dish is that if the eggs still look slightly undercooked on top when you remove them from the oven, that's a good thing — they'll keep cooking in the hot tomatoes and will be perfect by the time you serve them.

1 teaspoon coconut oil, plus extra for greasing
200 g (7 oz) tinned (or fresh) roma tomatoes, roughly chopped
2 handfuls of cherry tomatoes, halved
50 g (1¾ oz/1 cup firmly packed) baby spinach leaves
4 eggs
2 tablespoons labneh (goat's cheese or feta cheese also work well)
4 small sprigs of dill, or other soft herb of choice

Preheat the oven to 200°C (400°F). Warm a small frying pan over a medium heat and melt the coconut oil in it. Add all of the tomatoes and cook for 2 minutes, then remove from the heat.

Lightly grease four 250 ml (9 fl oz/1 cup) capacity ramekins with coconut oil. Divide the baby spinach and sautéed tomatoes evenly between the ramekins, then crack an egg into each nest of spinach and tomatoes. Place a dollop of labneh over each egg and top with a sprig of dill, then place the ramekins on a baking tray (baking sheet) and bake in the oven for 15–20 minutes. Once cooked, remove from the oven and let stand for 5 minutes before serving.

SERVES 4

BAKED EGGS
WITH SPINACH
AND LABNEH

This recipe is loosely based on one by Heidi Swanson, the Californian food writer and photographer who is one of my greatest inspirations when it comes to writing about, shooting and celebrating food. Her blog, *101 Recipes*, was the first I ever followed and it remains a never-ending source of beautiful imagery and creativity in words. I have to say thank you to this woman, who I've not met, for inspiring me and, without a doubt, so many others.

Sautéed kale with butterbeans, garlic and parmesan

GF / SF / V

2 tablespoons grapeseed
  or coconut oil
400 g (14 oz) cooked
  butterbeans (lima beans),
  either tinned, drained
  and rinsed or 190 g ($6\frac{3}{4}$ oz)
  dried beans, soaked
  and cooked
135 g ($4\frac{3}{4}$ oz/5 cups) roughly
  torn kale leaves
  (about $\frac{1}{2}$ a bunch)
2 garlic cloves, crushed
$\frac{1}{2}$ teaspoon finely grated
  lemon zest
a pinch of sea salt
juice of $\frac{1}{2}$ a lemon
freshly ground black pepper
2 tablespoons finely grated
  parmesan cheese

Warm the oil in a large frying pan over a medium heat. Add the butter beans and cook for 3 minutes. Add the kale leaves and mix them through the butter beans, cooking for a further 2 minutes. Stir through the garlic, lemon zest and salt and sauté for a final 2 minutes.

Remove from the heat, squeeze in the lemon juice, add a good grind of pepper and serve with the grated parmesan sprinkled over.

SERVES 4

Grilled mushrooms with tahini and chilli

GF / DF / SF / V / VG

Beautiful big field mushrooms add so much substance to a meal, whether it's breakfast, brunch, lunch or dinner. Their earthy flavours work wonderfully with the tahini.

4 large field mushrooms (about 200 g/7 oz each), stalks trimmed and gills brushed clean
2 teaspoons grapeseed oil
1 garlic clove, finely sliced
1 teaspoon oregano leaves, plus a few extra leaves, for garnish
4 lemon wedges
½ a bird's eye chilli, deseeded and finely chopped (optional)
sea salt and freshly ground black pepper
1 tablespoon tahini paste

Preheat the oven grill (broiler) to medium–high. Line a baking tray (baking sheet) with baking paper. Place the mushrooms, stalk side down, on the tray, Drizzle with the oil, then grill for approximately 8 minutes.

After 8 minutes, flip the mushrooms over and sprinkle over the garlic slices and oregano leaves. Cook for a further 2–3 minutes.

Remove from the grill and place each mushroom on a serving plate with a lemon wedge, a good pinch of fresh chilli (if using) and salt and pepper. Drizzle the tahini over the top, add a few more oregano leaves, and serve.

SERVES 4

Cinnamon, cardamom and orange tea

GF / DF / SF / V / VG

Cinnamon is so supportive for managing blood glucose levels and energy. Make a pot of this tea as your brunch is winding down; it's a lovely way to stabilise energy levels and relax into the next phase of the day.

4 cinnamon sticks
2 teaspoons cardamom pods
4 orange slices, washed well, peel left on
1 litre (35 fl oz/4 cups) boiling water

Combine all of the ingredients in a teapot and add the boiling water. Allow the tea to steep for at least 3–4 minutes, then serve.

SERVES 4

CINNAMON, CARDAMON
AND ORANGE TEA

GRILLED MUSHROOMS
WITH TAHINI AND CHILLI

A good homemade loaf is serious comfort food, and if you bring one that's still warm from the oven to the table for your guests to enjoy, they'll love it. The more you play with wholefood loaf variations, the more you will realise how easy and delightful they are to make and eat. I'll generally make a loaf on the weekend to accompany our breakfast or brunch and then use any leftovers in lunchboxes during the week. This loaf is naturally pretty moist, so even after a day or two in the fridge you can toast it and the flavours and texture will be sensational.

Pumpkin, carrot and herb loaf

GF / DF / SF / V

165 g (5¾ oz/1½ cups) quinoa flour

1 teaspoon sea salt

45 g (1¼ oz/¼ cup) chia seeds

40 g (1½ oz/¼ cup) sunflower seeds, plus extra for the top (optional)

40 g (1½ oz/¼ cup) pepitas (pumpkin seeds), plus extra for the top (optional)

15 g (½ oz/¼ cup) nutritional yeast (optional)

3 teaspoons aluminium- and gluten-free baking powder

125 ml (4 fl oz/½ cup) coconut oil, melted

4 eggs, beaten

a large handful of finely chopped mixed herbs, such as dill, basil and parsley

225 g (8 oz/1½ cups) diced (winter squash), roasted and cooled

150 g (5½ oz/1 cup) grated carrot (about 2 medium carrots)

Serve with butter or nut butter, tahini paste, ricotta cheese or avocado

Preheat the oven to 180°C (350°F) and line a 12 × 24 cm (4½ × 9½ inch) loaf (bar) tin with baking paper.

In a large mixing bowl, combine the quinoa flour, salt, chia seeds, sunflower seeds, pepitas, nutritional yeast and baking powder. In another bowl, mix together the coconut oil, eggs and herbs and whisk well to combine. Add this mixture to the dry ingredients, combine well, then fold through the cooked pumpkin and carrot so everything is well-combined but not overmixed.

Pour this mixture into the lined loaf tin, give it a little jiggle to help everything settle evenly, sprinkle with the extra sunflower seeds and pepitas, if using, and bake in the oven for 1 hour and 15 minutes, or until a skewer inserted into the centre comes out clean. Allow to cool in the tin for 10 minutes before removing, then leave on a wire rack to cool a little more.

Serve warm, with your choice of spread.

MAKES 1 LOAF, WHICH YIELDS ABOUT 10–12 SLICES

Bee pollen is a really special ingredient. It is the food created for young bees by the hive, and it is rich in amino acids and vitamins (particularly B complex). Bee pollen is great for digestion and for giving us energy, reducing inflammation in the respiratory system and supporting the cardiovascular system. You can find it in good health-food stores.

Salted caramel smoothie with bee pollen

GF / DF / SF / V

60 g (2¼ oz/½ cup)
  walnut halves
½ teaspoon vanilla paste
  or a pinch of
  vanilla powder
2 Medjool dates, pitted
a pinch of ground
  cinnamon
1 tablespoon coconut nectar
  or maple syrup
1 tablespoon chia seeds
2 teaspoons maca powder
a pinch of sea salt
2 teaspoons bee pollen,
  for the top

Place all the ingredients except the bee pollen in a blender and add 500 ml (17 fl oz/2 cups) of water. Blitz until smooth, then serve over ice with the bee pollen sprinkled on top.

SERVES 4 AS SHOTS OR TASTERS

for the boys

When I first started practising as a
nutritionist and running The Brown Paper
Bag, I noticed that the majority of my
clients were female. I know plenty of men
who are just as interested in their health and
diet, but the feedback from many of them was
that they didn't want to be bored eating 'just
salads' and that healthy food didn't always
satisfy their hunger. With this in mind,
I wanted to prove them wrong and really
show that a wholefoods diet could be intensely
flavoursome, nutritious *and* filling, while
also providing a good hit of the foods they
typically crave. It was also an opportunity
to teach a more balanced way of eating.

All of the menus in this book have been
created to offer something for everyone, but
this one in particular was developed using all
the things that I believe guys love to eat. So,
boys, without further ado, this one's for you.

SERVES 4

MAINS

SLOW-COOKED
BEEF BRISKET WITH
SMOKY HOMEMADE
BARBECUE SAUCE

CRISPY PORK BELLY
WITH PEAR CHUTNEY

SIDES

KALE AND RED
CABBAGE SLAW WITH
GINGER DRESSING

BEETROOT, BUCKWHEAT
AND WALNUT SALAD

ROSEMARY AND THYME
ROASTED POTATOES
AND PARSNIPS

CHILLI BAKED
CAULIFLOWER

SWEET

SELF-SAUCING
CHOCOLATE PUDDING

Brisket is quite a tough boneless piece of meat from the breast of the cow. Often it comes with a considerable amount of fat on it, which isn't desirable in this instance, so have your butcher trim some off. This cut is at its most delicious when slow-cooked, so get it in the oven on the morning of the day you plan on serving it. Here, Southern-style flavours with a good hit of chilli are used to create a spice rub for a seriously intense experience. The smoky barbecue sauce tops it off beautifully.

Slow-cooked beef brisket with smoky barbecue sauce

GF / DF   SMOKY BARBECUE SAUCE GF / DF

800 g (1 lb 12 oz) beef brisket
2 garlic cloves
1 onion, halved

For the spice rub
80 g (2¾ oz/½ cup)
   coconut sugar
1 teaspoon chilli powder
1 tablespoon smoked paprika
1 teaspoon sea salt
½ teaspoon black pepper
1 teaspoon cayenne pepper
½ tablespoon yellow
   mustard seeds
1 teaspoon ground cinnamon
2 teaspoons ground cumin

Smoky barbecue sauce
2 tablespoons grapeseed oil
1 onion, finely diced
1 x 400 g (14 oz) tin of tomatoes
40 g (1½ oz/¼ cup) coconut sugar
125 ml (4 fl oz/½ cup) apple
   cider vinegar
60 g (2¼ oz/¼ cup) dijon
   mustard
2 tablespoons tamari
1 teaspoon dried oregano
2 anchovy fillets
1 teaspoon smoked paprika

I like to start this recipe the night before and get the spice rub made and onto the meat, so it's ready to pull out of the fridge and slow-cook the next morning. In a small bowl, combine all of the ingredients for the spice rub. Rub this mixture all over the brisket so it is completely covered.

The next morning, take the brisket out of the fridge about an hour before cooking to allow it to come up to room temperature. Preheat the oven to 150°C (300°F).

Arrange the garlic and onion in the middle of a large casserole dish then place the brisket on top. Pour 750 ml (26 fl oz/3 cups) of water around the meat then put the lid on, or cover with a double layer of foil, and cook in the oven for 8 hours.

Make the barbecue sauce while the meat cooks. Heat the oil in a medium saucepan, add the onion and sauté for 4–5 minutes, or until softened. Add the remaining ingredients and simmer on low,

uncovered, for 40 minutes, stirring every now and then.

Once the sauce is nice and thick, take the pan off the heat and allow to cool for 10 minutes, then blitz in a blender until smooth. Allow to cool to room temperature, then pour into a clean airtight bottle or jar. (This sauce is also delicious with eggs in the morning or as a sauce for homemade baked beans. It will keep for about 2 weeks in the fridge.)

Once the brisket is perfectly cooked, discard the onion and garlic and move the meat to a chopping board. You can serve the brisket by leaving it whole, on the serving platter, and let your friends dig in, or shred it for them and serve it in a large bowl, or divided between plates. Serve next to a little bowl or jar of the smoky barbecue sauce.

SERVES 4-6
BARBECUE SAUCE MAKES 500 ML
(17 FL OZ/2 CUPS)

Ask your butcher to score the fat on the pork quite deeply — not enough to cut the meat underneath, but deep enough to get through the fat. If you need to do this at home, use a Stanley knife or your sharpest knife. When I first made this, I didn't score the skin deeply enough and the crackling didn't crisp up as evenly, or as much, as I wanted it to. So disappointing! The next time, I tried a deeper score and it worked a treat. Drying the skin out is also a crucial step to get that perfect crackling, so don't skip the steps below. You'll need to start this recipe the day before serving, so keep that in mind when planning your time.

Crispy pork belly with pear chutney

GF / DF   PEAR CHUTNEY GF / DF / V / VG

800 g (1 lb 12 oz) pork belly, fat scored (see recipe introduction)
1 tablespoon sesame oil
1 tablespoon sea salt

Dry marinade
40 g ($1\frac{1}{2}$ oz/$\frac{1}{4}$ cup) coconut sugar
2 tablespoons garam masala
1 teaspoon sea salt (additional)
1 teaspoon hot paprika

Pear chutney
500 g (1 lb 2 oz) pears, peeled, seeded and roughly chopped
1 onion, chopped into small pieces
125 ml (4 fl oz/$\frac{1}{2}$ cup) apple cider vinegar
80 g ($2\frac{3}{4}$ oz/$\frac{1}{2}$ cup) coconut sugar
$\frac{1}{2}$ teaspoon ground coriander
1 teaspoon yellow mustard seeds
a good pinch of sea salt

The day before, ensure the fat on the pork is well scored, then place the belly, skin side up, on a rack over the sink. Carefully pour 500 ml (17 fl oz/2 cups) of boiling water over the pork to scald the skin. Let it cool enough to touch, then dry the skin really well with paper towels and place the pork in a container in the fridge, uncovered, for 3 hours.

While the pork is drying, mix together the dry marinade ingredients and set aside.

Remove the pork from the fridge and, with the skin facing up, stab the skin several times using the tip of a sharp knife. Turn the pork over and cut diagonal incisions into the flesh approximately 2 cm ($\frac{3}{4}$ inch) long and 1 cm ($\frac{1}{2}$ inch) deep. Rub the marinade into the flesh only, massaging it into the incisions really well.

Place the pork back in the container, skin side up, and return to the fridge overnight, uncovered. This ensures the skin dries out really well so the crackling will become deliciously crisp.

The next day, about 1 hour prior to cooking, take the pork out of the fridge to come up to room temperature. Preheat the oven to 150°C (300°F).

Place the pork, still on the rack, over a roasting tin and rub the skin with the sesame oil and salt. Roast for 2 hours.

While the pork is cooking, make your chutney. Place all of the ingredients in a small saucepan, cover with a lid and bring to the boil. Reduce the heat and simmer, uncovered, for another hour to allow the fruit to become lovely and rich. Stir occasionally.

After 2 hours, increase the oven temperature to 220°C (425°F) and roast the pork for a further 15–20 minutes to puff up the skin for crackling. Remove from the oven and rest for 15 minutes before slicing and serving next to the pear chutney and some kale and cabbage slaw (see page opposite).

SERVES 4
PEAR CHUTNEY MAKES 310 ML ($10\frac{3}{4}$ FL OZ/$1\frac{1}{4}$ CUPS)

Vegetables in the brassica family, such as cabbage, kale, mustards, broccoli and cauliflower, are rich in sulphur compounds, which aid the body's natural detox pathways. These detoxifying ingredients are brought together in a delicious slaw and complemented with a ginger dressing that works like magic with the pork belly opposite.

Kale and red cabbage slaw with ginger dressing

GF / DF / SF / V / VG

Slaw
$\frac{1}{4}$ of a red cabbage, shredded
2 large kale leaves, stalks
   discarded, shredded
2 spring onions (scallions),
   white parts only,
   julienned
1 small green apple,
   julienned
a handful of mint leaves
a handful of coriander
   (cilantro), leaves whole
   and stalks finely chopped
a pinch of sea salt

Ginger dressing
1 tablespoon tamari
1 tablespoon lemon juice
2 teaspoons finely
   grated ginger
2 teaspoons apple
   cider vinegar
2 teaspoons extra virgin
   olive oil
1 shallot (eschalot),
   finely diced

Combine all of the slaw ingredients in a large bowl and toss gently.
   Combine all of the dressing ingredients in a small bowl and mix well. Add to the slaw and toss lightly just before serving.

SERVES 4

Buckwheat and beetroots have wonderful grounding properties — they nourish and balance — which is something I love about this salad. It's great as is, for a filling lunch, or you can serve it with protein such as a chicken breast or fish fillet. If you don't follow a dairy-free diet, you can also add some feta or goat's cheese for an extra hit of deliciousness.

Beetroot, buckwheat and walnut salad

GF / DF / SF / V / VG

½ a small red onion, finely sliced

50 g (1¾ oz/¼ cup) raw buckwheat, rinsed

1 red capsicum (pepper), seeded and finely sliced in long strips

a handful of flat-leaf (Italian) parsley, leaves picked, stalks finely chopped

60 g (2¼ oz/½ cup) walnuts, roughly chopped

75 g (2¾ oz/½ cup) currants

2 tablespoons extra virgin olive oil

1 tablespoon lemon juice

sea salt and freshly ground black pepper

1 beetroot (beet), peeled and grated

Place the onion in a small container of water and soak for 30 minutes to take the bitter onion flavour away, then drain.

To cook the buckwheat, bring a large saucepan of water to the boil. Add the rinsed buckwheat, place the lid on and bring back to the boil (this will take approximately 2 minutes), then cook for 12–15 minutes. This is a boiling rather than absorption method of cooking the buckwheat, so ensure you have plenty of water in your pan. Once cooked, drain the buckwheat and set aside.

Drain and rinse the onion, then combine with the buckwheat, capsicum, parsley, walnuts, currants, olive oil and lemon juice in a bowl, and toss together. Season with salt and pepper, then lightly toss through the beetroot and serve.

SERVES 4

Rosemary and thyme roasted potatoes and parsnips

GF / DF / SF / V / VG

Parsnips are an awesome way to vary a simple bowl of roasted potatoes or chips. They're rich in potassium and folate, which supports cardiac and muscle function, and fuel your body with lots of good energy.

250 g (9 oz) parsnips
250 g (9 oz) potatoes
1 tablespoon grapeseed or coconut oil
1 garlic clove, crushed
2 teaspoons finely chopped rosemary leaves
2 teaspoons finely chopped thyme leaves
sea salt

Preheat the oven to 200°C (400°F) and line a large baking tray (baking sheet) with baking paper.

Cut the parsnips and potatoes into 5 cm (2 inch) pieces about 1 cm (½ inch) thick.

Toss the parsnips and potatoes in the oil, garlic and herbs. Spread out on the tray and roast for 30 minutes, tossing after 10 and 20 minutes to ensure they are evenly roasted. Season well with salt and serve.

SERVES 4

Chilli baked cauliflower

GF / DF / SF / V / VG

Cauliflower is one of the most underrated vegetables and when it's roasted, it's definitely one of the best. It goes soft and creamy, just like potatoes, but harnesses a lot more nutrition than the humble spud. In particular, cauliflower boasts sulphur-containing chemicals known as glucosinolates. These compounds are responsible for protecting our bodies from inflammation, viral and bacterial infections, and damage to the DNA in our cells. They also promote liver detoxification. The fact that cauliflower tastes great is just a bonus.

½ a head of cauliflower, cut into florets
1 tablespoon grapeseed oil or ghee
¼ teaspoon chilli flakes
2 teaspoons ground cumin
a large handful of flat-leaf (Italian) parsley leaves
sea salt and freshly ground black pepper

Preheat the oven to 200°C (400°F) and line a baking tray (baking sheet) with baking paper.

Toss the cauliflower in the oil, chilli and cumin and roast for 30 minutes. Sprinkle over the parsley leaves, season well with salt and pepper and serve.

SERVES 4

CHILLI BAKED CAULIFLOWER

The size of the baking dish is quite important for this pudding as it affects the final 'saucing' result. If the dish is too large, the sauce is absorbed in the cooking process and your friends won't get to enjoy a gooey, chocolaty pudding, so up your quantities accordingly or pull the pudding out earlier to ensure a great result. It's absolutely insane served with a big dollop of Greek-style yoghurt, or cream if you're feeling super decadent. Pop the dish in the middle of the table and just let everyone tuck in!

Self-saucing chocolate pudding

Pudding batter

125 ml (4 fl oz/½ cup) coconut oil, melted and slightly cooled, plus extra for greasing

145 g (5 oz/1 cup) spelt flour

60 g (2¼ oz/½ cup) raw cacao powder

80 g (2¾ oz/½ cup) coconut sugar

2 teaspoons gluten- and aluminium-free baking powder

125 ml (4 fl oz/½ cup) plant-based milk, such as almond, coconut, rice or oat milk

1 egg, lightly beaten

Chocolate sauce

120 g (4¼ oz/¾ cup) coconut sugar

30 g (1 oz/¼ cup) raw cacao powder, sifted

Serve with raw cashew and coconut ice cream (see page 156), whipped coconut cream or Greek-style yoghurt

Preheat the oven to 180°C (350°F). Grease a 16 x 24 cm (6¼ x 9½ inch) dish with coconut oil.

Sift the flour and cacao into a large bowl, then stir in the coconut sugar and baking powder.

Combine the melted coconut oil, milk and egg in a small jug. Slowly add this to the flour mixture, whisking as you go, until well combined and smooth. Spoon the pudding batter into the baking dish and smooth the top.

To make the chocolate sauce, sprinkle the coconut sugar and cacao over the pudding. Slowly pour 310 ml (10¾ fl oz/1¼ cups)

of boiling water over the back of a large metal spoon to cover the pudding (doing this ensures the water is spread around the pudding). Place the dish onto a baking tray (baking sheet) and bake for 35–40 minutes, or until the pudding bounces back when pressed gently in the centre.

Serve straight from the dish for everyone to dig into, accompanied by your choice of raw ice cream, whipped coconut cream or Greek-style yoghurt.

SERVES 4-6

my Japanese feast
itadakimasu

When I was 10 years old, my family upped
and moved to Japan for a few years. Of all
the experiences I had in my childhood, I think
living in Japan tops them all. Of course at the
time I was apprehensive about moving to a
country where I had no friends, didn't speak the
language or understand the culture, but once we
arrived I couldn't have felt more welcomed by
our Japanese neighbours and new friends.

We lived in the ward of Shibuya-Ku in
the heart of Tokyo, and would ride our bikes
to the local food haunts and markets.
On a daily basis we'd shop for groceries in our
neighbourhood, Hiroo. As we did, I'd use my
evolving understanding of the language to speak
to the grocers until eventually I felt totally
immersed in Japanese food, spirituality and
culture. I learned to say '*itadakimasu*' before
eating my meals, like many of the locals. Loosely
translated, it's a sort of blessing, or thanks for
the food. Those grocers and market vendors
inspired me to learn through food in a way I'd
never experienced, and for that, I will always
be grateful.

So much of my cooking now is heavily
influenced by my time in Japan and the flavours
I learned to love there. I've tried to capture as
much of those memories in this Japanese feast,
but honestly I think I could write a whole book
about it. Maybe someday I will. Until then,
itadakimasu!

SERVES 4

**SMALL BITES
TO START**

PUMPKIN AND GINGER
DUMPLINGS

EDAMAME ROLLS

RED QUINOA
VEGETARIAN SUSHI

SIDES

WASABI PEA SALAD

RAW ZUCCHINI NOODLE
SALAD WITH CORIANDER

WARM MUSHROOM
AND PINE NUT SALAD
WITH BABY SPINACH

MAINS

BLACK SESAME
TERIYAKI CHICKEN

MISO-GLAZED TROUT

SWEET

SESAME HONEY MOCHI

My Japanese language teacher, Naoko, brought these little dumplings into our lives. They're such a humble mouthful of ginger and pumpkin. Ginger supports the body's circulatory system and is a wonderful thing to integrate into the diet as the months become cooler.

Pumpkin and ginger dumplings

GF / DF / SF / V / VG

500 g (1 lb 2 oz) pumpkin
    (winter squash), peeled
    and roughly diced
2 teaspoons coconut oil,
    melted
40 g (1½ oz/¼ cup) sesame
    seeds, plus extra seeds
    toasted, to serve
a pinch of sea salt
2 teaspoons finely
    grated ginger
1 tablespoon tamari
2 tablespoons coconut flour

Garnish with chopped
    chives or coriander
    (cilantro) leaves and
    serve with tamari
    (optional)

Bring a large saucepan of water to the boil and insert a steamer basket or large sieve inside it, making sure it does not touch the water below. Add the pumpkin, then cover and steam until very soft. Remove from the steamer and mash with a fork.

While the pumpkin is steaming, warm the coconut oil in a small frying pan on a medium heat. Add the sesame seeds and salt, and toast until the seeds are golden brown.

Mix the mashed pumpkin, ginger, tamari, half of the sesame seeds and coconut flour together in a bowl. Scoop 1½ tablespoons of the mix into a small piece of plastic wrap and shape into a dumpling by gently squeezing together into a teardrop shape. Place the dumplings on a tray or plate as you go, still in the plastic wrap. (You should get 12 from this much mixture.)

Put the dumplings in the fridge for 30 minutes before unwrapping them. Once unwrapped, sprinkle with the remaining toasted sesame seeds. Serve chilled, garnished with some chopped chives or coriander leaves sprinkled on top and some tamari for dipping, if you like.

MAKES 12

Photograph page 186

Rice paper rolls aren't traditionally a part of Japanese cuisine but I love fusing different cuisines when it feels right, and here they play well with edamame (young soya beans in their pods). You can buy edamame fresh or frozen, podded or still in their shells. This is one of my son's favourite things to eat when we have an Asian-inspired dinner at home, so that's enough reason for me to include it. Love you, Jet!

Edamame rolls

GF / DF / SF / V / VG

Edamame filling

150 g (5½ oz/1 cup) shelled
  edamame beans
½ teaspoon finely grated
  lime zest
1 tablespoon coconut oil
1 tablespoon coconut cream
  or coconut milk
2 teaspoons lime juice
2 spring onions (scallions),
  white and green parts
  roughly chopped
a pinch of sea salt

16 small rice paper
  wrappers
a small handful of
  mint leaves
a small handful of snow
  pea (mangetout) sprouts

Serve with tamari
  (optional)

Bring a medium saucepan of water to the boil and cook the edamame beans until tender, approximately 10 minutes. Drain them, then blitz until smooth with the rest of the filling ingredients in a blender. Put the mixture in the fridge to set for 4 hours.

To make the rolls, working one at a time, dip a rice paper wrapper into a bowl of hot water for 20 seconds until softened, then remove and keep flat on a board. Place one mint leaf in the middle of the wrap, add 2 tablespoons of the edamame filling and top with a pinch of snow pea (mangetout) sprouts. Roll the bottom edge up, fold in each side, and then finish by rolling up tightly. Repeat with the remaining wrappers. Keep the rolls as fresh as possible by storing them in the fridge in an airtight container lined with a damp tea towel.

Serve as they are, or with a small dipping bowl of tamari.

MAKES 16 ROLLS

BLACK SESAME
TERIYAKI CHICKEN
recipe page 190

WASABI PEA SALAD
recipe page 189

Quinoa is not typically a Japanese ingredient, but it's a healthier alternative to the usual sticky white sushi rice and also ups the protein content of these rolls. The nutty flavour of the quinoa goes beautifully with the other ingredients, and adds an extra dimension of flavour and texture that I really love.

Red quinoa vegetarian sushi

GF / DF / SF / V / VG

100 g ($3\frac{1}{2}$ oz/$\frac{1}{2}$ cup) red quinoa, rinsed and drained

110 g ($3\frac{3}{4}$ oz/$\frac{1}{2}$ cup) brown rice, rinsed and drained

a pinch of sea salt

1 teaspoon apple cider vinegar

1 avocado, peeled and diced into small cubes

4 toasted nori sheets

$\frac{1}{2}$ a red capsicum (pepper), julienned

$\frac{1}{2}$ a carrot, julienned

small handful of watercress, leaves picked

4 coriander (cilantro) sprigs

Serve with tamari and wasabi paste

Put the rinsed quinoa and rice in a small saucepan with 750 ml (26 fl oz/3 cups) of water. Place over a medium–high heat, cover the saucepan and bring to the boil. Once boiling, remove the lid and continue to cook at a fast simmer until all the liquid has been absorbed, about 20 minutes, then aside to cool.

Add the salt, apple cider vinegar and diced avocado to the quinoa–rice combination. Mix well and then press it with the back of a fork so it binds together, like sushi rice would.

Lay a sheet of nori, shiny side down, on a large chopping board. If you have a sushi mat, that will make it easier to roll these. With the lines of the sushi mat running horizontally, spread a quarter of the quinoa-rice mixture over the entire sheet of nori and press down again with the back of the fork to ensure the mix sticks to the nori. Place a quarter of the capsicum, carrot, watercress and coriander about 3 cm ($1\frac{1}{4}$ inches) up from the bottom edge.

Starting with the edge closest to you, begin to tightly roll all the way to the end. Using your fingers, press the roll together firmly to create a rectangular-shaped roll. With a sharp knife, cut the roll into 6 equal pieces. Repeat this process with the remaining quinoa, nori and vegetables until you have 24 pieces of sushi.

Arrange on a serving platter and serve with tamari and wasabi.

MAKES 24 SMALL PIECES OF SUSHI

Photograph page 186

Peas aren't really fresh seasonal autumm produce, but the ones you buy from a store freezer are frozen within hours of being picked, so if you're going to eat any ingredient out of season, peas are the ones to choose! They are so tasty that I tend to keep a bag in the freezer and work them into any dishes I can. The delicious sweet morsels in this salad are given a real kick thanks to the wasabi paste and zesty lemon finish. Be sure not to overcook the peas as they will lose their colour, and the bright green hues are a vital component of our Japanese table.

Wasabi pea salad

GF / DF / SF / V / VG

425 g (15 oz/3 cups) frozen
   peas, blanched
2 nori sheets, finely
   chopped to produce
   $\frac{1}{4}$ cup (this is easiest
   done with scissors)
2 tablespoons sesame seeds,
   toasted
2 baby red radishes,
   julienned

Dressing
2 teaspoons wasabi paste
1 tablespoon lemon juice
1 teaspoon finely grated
   lemon zest
2 tablespoons extra virgin
   olive oil
freshly ground
   black pepper

In a large mixing bowl combine the peas, chopped nori, sesame seeds and radish.

Combine the dressing ingredients in a small bowl. Drizzle over the salad right before serving and toss gently to coat all of the ingredients. Transfer to a shallow serving bowl and take to the table.

SERVES 4

Photograph page 187

Black sesame teriyaki chicken

GF / DF / SF

400 g (14 oz) skinless chicken breasts
¾ teaspoon sesame oil

Teriyaki marinade
1 teaspoon finely grated ginger
2 large garlic cloves, crushed
1 tablespoon sesame oil
2 tablespoons apple cider vinegar
2 tablespoons rice malt syrup or
   1 tablespoon maple syrup
80 ml (2½ fl oz/⅓ cup) tamari

*Serve with blanched kale leaves (tough stems
   removed) and 1 teaspoon of black sesame seeds*

To make the teriyaki marinade, place all of the
ingredients in a jar, shake well and set aside.
If you are using rice malt syrup, which is thicker
than maple syrup, you may wish to whisk the
marinade in a bowl instead.

   Slice the chicken breasts into large pieces.
Place in a shallow dish and pour the marinade
all over the chicken, so all of the pieces are
completely coated. Leave to marinate for at least
5–10 minutes.

   Heat a large frying pan on a high heat. Add the
sesame oil, then the marinated chicken and any
marinade left in the dish. Stir-fry for 3–4 minutes,
or until the thickest slice of chicken is cooked
through. Remove from the pan and serve on a
bed of blanched kale leaves with the black sesame
seeds sprinkled over the top.

SERVES 4

Raw zucchini noodle salad with coriander

GF / DF / SF / V / VG

Salad
1 large zucchini (courgette)
2 spring onions (scallions), white parts only,
   finely chopped
a small handful of coriander (cilantro),
   leaves and stalks finely chopped
50 g (1¾ oz/1 cup) baby spinach leaves
1 teaspoon white sesame seeds, toasted
2 lemon wedges, to serve

Dressing
1 teaspoon tamari
1 teaspoon apple cider vinegar
1 tablespoon sesame oil
1 tablespoon olive oil
1 tablespoon pickled ginger, finely chopped
   (see note below)

Combine all of the dressing ingredients in a jar,
shake well, then set aside.

   To make the zucchini noodles, use a vegetable
peeler to slice down the full length of the zucchini,
rotating the zucchini as you go so the ribbons are
similar in size. Once done, thinly slice the ribbons
into noodles. If you have a spiraliser at home, by
all means, use that!

   Combine the zucchini noodles, spring onions,
coriander and spinach in a bowl, pour over the
dressing and toss to combine.

   Sprinkle the sesame seeds over the top and
serve with lemon wedges.

NOTE

Aim to buy organic pickled white ginger wherever
possible as opposed to pink ginger, which is dyed.

SERVES 4

Mushrooms, in particular shiitakes, contain a bounty of nourishing properties that support the immune system. Shiitake has been used medicinally in Japan and much of Asia for thousands of years. Its powerful component is lentinan, which strengthens the immune system to fight infection and disease.

Warm mushroom and pine nut salad with baby spinach

GF / DF / SF / V / VG

Salad

3 tablespoons grapeseed oil

400 g (14 oz) mixed mushrooms such as oyster, shiitake and shimeji, brushed clean

40 g (1½ oz/¼ cup) pine nuts, toasted

40 g (1½ oz/¼ cup) sesame seeds, toasted

100 g (3½ oz) bok choy (pak choy), trimmed and finely sliced

1 tablespoon dried wakame, soaked in water for 4 minutes, then drained

50 g (1¾ oz/1 cup) baby spinach leaves

2 spring onions (scallions), white parts only, finely sliced

Dressing

1 tablespoon lime juice

½ teaspoon finely chopped bird's eye chilli

1 tablespoon olive oil

1 teaspoon apple cider vinegar

2 teaspoons tamari

½ garlic clove, crushed

sea salt and freshly ground black pepper

Garnish with a few sprigs of microherbs or coriander (cilantro) leaves

Combine all of the dressing ingredients in a jar, shake well then set aside.

Warm the grapeseed oil in a large frying pan on a medium heat, then add the mushrooms. Turn the heat up to high and cook, ensuring the mushrooms are evenly coated with the oil, for 2 minutes. Remove from the heat and allow to cool ever so slightly, then add half of the pine nuts and sesame seeds and stir gently.

Arrange half of the bok choy, wakame, spinach and spring onion on a serving plate. Top with half of the mushroom mixture and repeat the process, finishing with the remaining pine nuts and sesame seeds.

Drizzle over the dressing and serve garnished with a sprinkling of herbs.

SERVES 4

Miso is a fermented soya bean paste that is rich in probiotics, making it great for gut health and therefore digestion and immunity. Miso's salty taste combines beautifully with the other marinade ingredients here to create not only a sensational flavour and stunning glazed finish, but also one of the most succulent pieces of fish you'll ever eat! My top tip is to marinate the trout overnight. This creates a beautiful caramelised finish. If you do this, just up the cooking time by a few minutes. The zucchini salad on page 190 is the perfect complement.

Miso-glazed trout

GF / DF / SF

400 g (14 oz) trout fillets (approximately 2 large fillets), skin on and pinboned

Miso marinade
1 tablespoon white miso paste
1 tablespoon apple cider vinegar
1 tablespoon sesame oil
1 tablespoon maple syrup
2 teaspoons tamari

Serve with sesame seeds and lemon wedges

Preheat the oven to 180°C (350°F) and line a baking tray (baking sheet) with baking paper.

Combine all of the ingredients for the marinade in a small bowl and whisk well. Evenly coat the trout with the marinade and rub it all over the flesh.

Place the trout, skin side down, on the baking tray and bake in the oven for 8 minutes (12 if you marinated overnight) while you

prepare the zucchini noodle salad (if making).

Remove the trout from the oven and allow to rest for a couple of minutes, covered with foil.

When you are ready to serve, sprinkle the fish with sesame seeds and serve with wedges of lemon and a good helping of the zucchini noodle salad.

SERVES 4

There are plenty of beautiful sweets in Japanese culture, but one stands out in my memory as it was often gifted or presented to me for dessert. 'Mochi' are pounded rice balls with a sweet red bean paste filling. They are often coated with sesame seeds and are the inspiration for this recipe. My mochi recipe contains neither rice nor bean paste, but it manages to capture those delightful mouthfuls and the smooth, sweet sesame flavours I remember so well. The enjoyment of food is just as much about memorable experiences and moments as it is the food itself.

Sesame honey mochi

GF / DF / SF / V

190 g ($6\frac{3}{4}$ oz/$1\frac{1}{4}$ cups) raw
  cashews
55 g (2 oz/$\frac{3}{4}$ cup)
  shredded coconut
2 tablespoons raw honey
2 tablespoons unhulled
  tahini
125 ml (4 fl oz/$\frac{1}{2}$ cup)
  coconut milk
$\frac{1}{2}$ teaspoon vanilla powder
  or extract
a small handful of black
  or white sesame seeds

Place all of the ingredients (except the sesame seeds) in a food processor and blitz until well combined. Transfer to a bowl and place in the fridge for 20–30 minutes to allow the mixture to harden slightly before rolling.

Pour enough sesame seeds onto a large plate to cover the base. Decide how large you want the balls to be (a tablespoon for snack size or a teaspoon for toothpick size) and make one ball at a time. Spoon some of the mixture into the palm of your hand, gently roll into a round, then roll in the sesame seeds until completely coated. Place on a tray and return to the fridge until ready to serve. These will keep in an airtight container in the fridge for up to 2 weeks.

MAKES 12 SNACK-SIZE BALLS

winter

Winter is a different experience for all of us. Some relish the idea of layering up in woollies and getting out in the cold air; others crave the warmth of the spring just around the corner. Winter in Australia is never that cold, but for those in the northern hemisphere it is quite the opposite, so the key to creating, preparing and eating for the season is to do what suits the climate you live in. Do that, and your body will respond accordingly.

If the winter is temperate, create food that is a balance of heavier and lighter dishes. If it is cold, focus on a menu with heartier foods that have been cooked for longer. Heavier foods will warm the body, storing energy to nourish it throughout the winter months.

Winter occasions should be created with warmth in mind, too. Big rugs and woolly scarves folded over chairs for guests to wrap themselves in, fires burning, the smell of food roasting as guests walk through the door, rustic table settings that highlight and complement the dishes served, evenings that have no end in sight as you snuggle into a lover ... these are things that come to mind when I think of sharing meals during the winter months.

WINTER VEGETABLES

BEETROOT
  (BEETS)
BRUSSELS
  SPROUTS
CABBAGE
CARROT
CAVOLO NERO
CAULIFLOWER
CELERIAC
FENNEL
GARLIC
GINGER
GREEN BEANS
HORSERADISH
KALE
LEEK
OLIVE
PARSNIP
POTATO
PUMPKIN
SPINACH
SWEET POTATO
TURNIP
WITLOF
  (ENDIVE)

WINTER FRUITS

APPLE
AVOCADO
CUSTARD APPLE
GRAPEFRUIT
KIWI FRUIT
LEMON
LIME
MANDARIN
PASSIONFRUIT
PEAR
PERSIMMON
POMELO
QUINCE
RHUBARB

date night

Whether you've been married for 40 years or dating for four weeks, there's something special about preparing a beautifully considered, elaborate meal for that certain someone. Food made with love makes for romance at the table, and beyond. Date night at home shouldn't mean hours spent in the kitchen. The more you are present at the table being your wonderful charming self, the better, so it's important to plan dishes that can mostly be prepared ahead of time. Both of the desserts here can be made a few days in advance. That way, when the evening gets underway, you just need to add a little spark of this and that in the kitchen before serving. I've gone for flavours and ingredients that combine delicacy and tradition because I find those are the types of things guaranteed to touch the heart.

SERVES 2

APPETISER

OYSTERS WITH A
GINGER VINAIGRETTE

ENTRÉE

ZUCCHINI PASTA
WITH PRAWNS,
CHILLI AND LEMON

SIDE

MANDARIN, BEETROOT
AND RHUBARB SALAD

MAIN

STUFFED ROASTED
CHICKEN MARYLANDS
ON CARROT AND
THYME PURÉE

DESSERT

STICKY DATE
PUDDINGS

NIGHT BITE

RAW CHOCOLATE
WITH SPICES
AND FIGS

STICKY DATE PUDDINGS (TOP RIGHT) *recipe page 208*

OYSTERS WITH A GINGER VINAIGRETTE (ABOVE LEFT) *recipe page 202*

ZUCCHINI PASTA WITH
PRAWNS, CHILLI AND LEMON
recipe page 203

Oysters and date night are a food match made in heaven, but only if you buy the freshest seafood you can get your hands on. Ask your fishmonger to clean and shuck the oysters for you when you buy them, leaving them on the half shell so you know you are getting the best of the best. Nothing ruins a hot date faster than dodgy seafood.

Oysters with a ginger vinaigrette

GF / DF / SF

6 fresh oysters, shucked
   and on the half shell
sea salt and freshly ground
   black pepper

Ginger vinaigrette
2 teaspoons finely
   grated ginger
2 teaspoons apple
   cider vinegar
2 teaspoons extra virgin
   olive oil
1 shallot (eschalot), peeled
   and finely diced
1 teaspoon lime juice

Garnish with microherbs
   such as baby radish
   or chervil

In a small bowl, mix all of the ingredients for the ginger vinaigrette together.

Carefully remove each oyster from its shell, place a teaspoon or so of vinaigrette in each of the oyster shells, then place the oyster back on top. Arrange on a platter, then season with a tiny pinch of salt and pepper, top with microherbs and eat right away.

SERVES 2

Photograph page 200

Zucchini pasta, also known as 'zoodles' or 'spirals', has become one of the best alternatives to wheat-based pasta due to the neutral flavour of the zucchini and its ability to hold its shape and soak up delicious flavours. There are plenty of tools around to make these zoodles, but you don't need fancy equipment or skill of any sort to get started. Simply use a vegetable peeler to make long thin strips of zucchini, then either keep them wide or stack them and cut lengthways into thinner strips.

Zucchini pasta with prawns, chilli and lemon

GF / DF / SF

2 large zucchini (courgettes)

3 tablespoons olive oil

6 raw king prawns, peeled and deveined (tails left on)

1 garlic clove, finely chopped

1 teaspoon finely grated lemon zest

$\frac{1}{2}$ teaspoon finely chopped red bird's eye chilli (seeds removed if you don't want the pasta too spicy)

2 tablespoons lemon juice

a small handful of rocket (arugula) leaves

60 g ($2\frac{1}{4}$ oz) freshly grated parmesan cheese (optional)

sea salt and freshly ground black pepper

To make the zucchini pasta, either use a spiraliser or follow the instructions in the introduction above. I prefer my noodles slightly thinner as I find they catch the flavours a bit better, but go with what you feel most comfortable with to start and progress to thinner noodles as your confidence improves. If you want to make these earlier in the day, they'll keep well in the fridge until you're ready to cook them.

Bring a large saucepan of water to the boil. Cook the zucchini noodles for 1 minute then remove from the pan and drain well.

Heat the olive oil in a large frying pan over a medium heat. Then add the prawns, garlic, lemon zest and chilli and cook, keeping everything moving around the pan, until the prawns just start to change colour. Add the drained zucchini noodles and toss well to combine. Gently stir through the lemon juice, rocket, grated parmesan (if using), and a good pinch of salt and pepper, then serve immediately.

SERVES 2

Photograph page 201

This is one of my favourite salads because it's where the flavours, colours and seasonal foods of winter unite. Rhubarb is usually cooked with copious amounts of sugar as a sweet item for breakfast or dessert, so it's nice to take it out of that pigeonhole and into a salad space. Let this be an opening for your creativity to flow and find new ways to use rhubarb. Once you start, the options are endless.

Mandarin, beetroot and rhubarb salad

GF / DF / SF / V / VG

1 beetroot (beet), unpeeled
1 rhubarb stalk, sliced
   approximately 4 cm
   (1½ inches) long on the
   diagonal
1 teaspoon rice malt syrup
a pinch of sea salt
1 mandarin
2 tablespoons finely
   shredded sorrel, baby
   spinach, silverbeet (Swiss
   chard) or rocket (arugula)

Dressing
½ teaspoon apple
   cider vinegar
½–1 teaspoon walnut oil
   (or extra virgin olive oil)
freshly ground
   black pepper

Preheat the oven to 200°C (400°F) and wrap the beetroot in foil. Bake in the oven for 30 minutes, then allow to cool before peeling off the skin (use rubber gloves if you don't want pink hands!).

While the beetroot is cooling, line a baking tray (baking sheet) with baking paper. Toss the rhubarb with the rice malt syrup and salt on the tray, then roast for 10 minutes. Remove from the oven and allow to cool for a few minutes.

Using a sharp knife, slice off the peel and white pith from the mandarin, then separate into individual segments.

Slice the cooled beetroot into wedges and arrange them on a plate with the rhubarb and the mandarin segments.

Combine the dressing ingredients, drizzle over the salad and top with the shredded greens.

SERVES 2

Chicken legs are humble and delicious, yet this is one of those meals that seems to be infrequently made. But it's not too challenging and it's rare that anything will go wrong, especially when the meat is hugged by a generous coating of herbs and spices. Be sure to let the chicken rest (covered) for five minutes or so after you take it out of the oven. The meat relaxes in this time, making it all the more succulent and also giving you a few minutes to plate up the other elements.

Stuffed roasted chicken marylands on carrot and thyme purée

GF / DF / SF

2 chicken marylands
 (leg quarters)
1 red onion, thickly sliced

Herby turmeric stuffing
1 garlic clove, finely sliced
1 bird's eye chilli, thinly
 sliced
3 tablespoons lemon juice
a large handful of flat-leaf
 (Italian) parsley, stalks
 and leaves finely chopped
a large handful of
 coriander (cilantro),
 leaves and stalks
 finely chopped
$\frac{1}{2}$ teaspoon ground
 turmeric
$\frac{1}{2}$ teaspoon ground cumin

Carrot and thyme purée
500g carrots, roughly
 chopped
1 teaspoon thyme leaves
1 garlic clove, skin on
1 tablespoon olive oil

A few hours before serving, start on the purée. Preheat the oven to 200°C (400°F) and line a baking tray (baking sheet) with baking paper. Toss the carrot with the thyme leaves, garlic and olive oil on the tray and roast in the oven for 30 minutes.

Once cooked, squeeze the garlic out of the skin (discard the skin) and place all of the ingredients for the purée in a food processor. Blitz until smooth. Transfer to a container, cover and put in the fridge until needed.

When you are ready to cook the chicken, preheat the oven to 180°C (350°F). Mix the stuffing ingredients together in a small bowl, reserving a few chilli slices and coriander leaves for garnish.

Lift the skin of the chicken gently and push the stuffing underneath the skin to coat the flesh as evenly as possible.

Place the red onion in a roasting tin and lay the chicken legs, skin side up, on top of the onion. Cover with foil, then roast in the oven for 30 minutes. Take off the foil, baste with any juices and cook for another 20 minutes, basting again halfway through if you can. Remove the chicken when the skin is lovely and golden and allow to rest, covered with foil, for 10 minutes.

While the chicken rests, gently reheat the carrot and thyme purée in a small saucepan over a medium–low heat. When ready to serve, spoon generous portions of the purée onto each plate and place a chicken leg on top, garnish with the reserved chilli and coriander, then take to the table.

SERVES 2

By the time dessert rolls around, your date will probably have already been seduced by the food — if not, he or she is about to be because these puddings win over hearts (and stomachs) without fail. The secret to this sticky date delight lies in its texture and the balanced sweetness with a beautiful creamy finish from the maple coconut sauce. If you make a bigger batch of these (just scale up the recipe accordingly), they will freeze really well, so you can either make some well in advance to keep date night simple, or make them on the day then have a few up your sleeve for impromptu dessert dates down the track.

Sticky date puddings

GF / DF

125 g (4½ oz) Medjool dates, pitted
¼ teaspoon bicarbonate of soda (baking soda)
1 tablespoon coconut oil, melted
1 egg, beaten
1 tablespoon coconut sugar
30 g (1 oz) almond meal
40 g (1½ oz/¼ cup) brown rice flour

Maple coconut sauce
125 ml (4 fl oz/½ cup) coconut cream
2 tablespoons maple syrup
½ teaspoon maca powder

Preheat the oven to 160°C (315°F) and line two 250 ml (9 fl oz/1 cup) capacity holes in a cupcake tin with paper cases or small square pieces of baking paper.

Put 3 tablespoons of water in a saucepan and add the dates. Bring to the boil then remove from the heat, stir in the bicarbonate of soda and allow to cool. Once cool, mash the dates into smaller pieces.

In a large mixing bowl, combine the coconut oil, egg, coconut sugar, almond meal and brown rice flour. Stir in the mashed dates. Spoon the mixture into the cases, then place the cupcake tin inside a roasting tin and pour in enough water to come about halfway up the outside of the cupcake tin. Bake in the oven for 20 minutes.

While the puddings cook, make the sauce. Gently heat the coconut cream in a small saucepan over a low heat and whisk in the maple syrup and maca powder. Heat gently for around 4–5 minutes. Carefully remove the puddings from their cases and serve with the warm maple coconut sauce drizzled generously on top.

NOTE

These puddings can be cooked earlier in the day and then just gently warmed in the oven while you eat the main course. The sauce can also be made ahead and warmed before serving.

SERVES 2

Photograph page 200

This raw chocolate works really well with any combination of fruits, nuts, seeds, spices or interesting superfood ingredient you wish to add. The base recipe is simply coconut oil, raw cacao powder and maple syrup, and from there it's choose your own adventure! This keeps really well in an airtight container for up to a week, so it makes a great after-dinner treat or snack when you need that hit of chocolate.

Raw chocolate with spices and figs

GF / DF / SF / V / VG

170 ml (5$\frac{1}{2}$ fl oz/$\frac{2}{3}$ cup)
  coconut oil
90 g (3$\frac{1}{4}$ oz/$\frac{3}{4}$ cup) raw
  cacao powder
2 tablespoons maple syrup
3 teaspoons ground
  cinnamon
1$\frac{1}{2}$ teaspoons ground
  nutmeg
1 teaspoon ground ginger
1 teaspoon maca powder
95 g (3$\frac{1}{4}$ oz/$\frac{1}{2}$ cup) dried figs,
  finely chopped
40 g (1$\frac{1}{2}$ oz/$\frac{1}{4}$ cup) currants

Line a 20 cm (8 inch) square cake tin with baking paper.

Place the coconut oil in a small saucepan over a low heat and melt. Remove from the heat and whisk in the cacao, maple syrup, spices, and maca. Once well blended, pour into the tin and gently tilt the tin from side-to-side to spread the chocolate out evenly.

Drop the figs and currants into the chocolate, then place in the refrigerator to set for 2 hours or more before serving. To serve, break off rough shards or cut into pieces and pile into a little bowl.

MAKES 1 LARGE 20 CM (8 INCH) SQUARE OF CHOCOLATE

When I lived in Italy as a uni student, I shared an apartment with three crazy Italian girls in Bologna. There was an incredible language barrier at the start, but we eventually found our way through it by uniting in the kitchen. Of all the foods I watched them cook, I loved their risottos the most. There is something so warming and comforting about risotto, and by using buckwheat rather than the traditional Arborio rice, it becomes even more wholesome and nourishing.

Mixed mushroom and buckwheat risotto

GF / DF / SF / V / VG

2 tablespoons grapeseed oil

1 onion, finely diced

3 garlic cloves, crushed

390 g (13¾ oz/2 cups) raw buckwheat

1.125 litres (39 fl oz/4½ cups) stock of your choice

200 g (7 oz/2 cups) mixed mushrooms, sliced

1 tablespoon thyme leaves, fresh or dried

sea salt and freshly ground black pepper

2 tablespoons nutritional yeast (or you can use 40 g (1½ oz/½ cup) freshly grated parmesan cheese if you aren't dairy-free or vegan)

Serve with 3 tablespoons of chopped flat-leaf (Italian) parsley leaves and a drizzle of truffle oil

Heat the oil in a large frying pan over a medium heat. Once hot, add the onion and garlic and sauté for a few minutes, until translucent. Add the buckwheat and stir until well coated in the oil and sautéed onion and garlic. Add 250 ml (9 fl oz/ 1 cup) of stock and simmer, lid off, on a medium heat until the liquid is absorbed.

Next, add the mushrooms and thyme leaves with another 250 ml of stock. Stir to combine and continue to simmer until the liquid is absorbed. Once absorbed, stir in a further 250 ml of stock.

Once again, simmer until the liquid is absorbed.

Add the remaining stock along with a good pinch of salt and pepper and the nutritional yeast. Continue to simmer, lid off, until the liquid has absorbed and the desired oozy consistency is reached.

Divide between serving bowls then sprinkle with some chopped parsley and a drizzle of truffle oil before serving.

SERVES 4-6

Every season should have its own signature bowl of greens to accompany a meal, and kale and silverbeet (Swiss chard) are two hardy winter greens that are packed with nutrients, and also really tasty when they're treated the right way. I'm using almond oil to accompany my winter greens, but extra virgin olive oil, macadamia, walnut or hazelnut oil would all work beautifully, too.

Steamed winter greens with pistachio, basil and goji berries

GF / DF / SF / V / VG

2 tablespoons goji berries

6 stalks of silverbeet (Swiss chard)

2 kale leaves, stalks discarded

3 tablespoons finely shredded basil leaves

35 g (1¼ oz/¼ cup) shelled pistachios, roughly chopped and lightly toasted

Dressing

1 teaspoon almond oil

½ teaspoon balsamic vinegar

sea salt and freshly ground black pepper

Soak the goji berries in water for 5–10 minutes to rehydrate them, then drain and set aside.

Bring a large saucepan of water with a steamer insert (or sieve) inside it to the boil. Make sure the water is not touching the steamer. Place the silverbeet and kale leaves in the steamer, then cover and steam for 2 minutes, or until tender.

Remove the leaves from the steamer and arrange them in layers on a serving plate with the basil, pistachios and goji berries sprinkled on top.

Combine the dressing ingredients. Drizzle all over the greens and then serve.

SERVES 4

Roasting the radicchio and olives intensifies their flavour and takes this warm salad to another level. This is all about deep, layered flavours and hearty ingredients. Think of it as the dark, moody cousin of a fresh summer salad.

Warm radicchio with quinoa and olives

GF / DF OPTION / SF / V

1 tablespoon grapeseed oil

1 red onion, cut into thin wedges

1 head of radicchio, cut into thin wedges

85 g (3 oz/½ cup) Sicilian green olives, cracked and pitted

sea salt and freshly ground black pepper

165 g (5¾ oz/1 cup) cooked quinoa

20 g (¾ oz/¼ cup) shaved parmesan (optional)

Maple balsamic dressing

2 teaspoons maple syrup

1 teaspoon balsamic vinegar

1 tablespoon extra virgin olive oil

Preheat the oven to 200°C (400°F) and line a roasting tin with baking paper. Drizzle the grapeseed oil all over the tray then toss the onion in the oil and roast in the oven for 20 minutes. Add the radicchio and olives, then return to the oven and roast for 5–10 minutes more.

Combine the dressing ingredients in a small bowl and set aside.

Arrange the radicchio, onion and olives on a serving platter and season well with salt and pepper. Scatter over the cooked quinoa and shaved parmesan, if using. Drizzle over the maple balsamic dressing and serve while still warm.

SERVES 4

The bone marrow found in this particular cut of meat really brings an extra dimension of flavour to this wonderful dish. Marrow is the fatty tissue in the core of the bone and it's high in the essential fatty acids, vitamins and minerals that support oxygen transport around the body, immunity, gut healing, bone strength and brain function. Despite these fantastic benefits, we don't use it enough, unless it's through slow-cooking or bone broths. So this is a great dish for those winter months, when we crave deep, hearty flavours and are in need of a nutritional boost.

Osso bucco with cauliflower purée

GF / DF / SF

Osso bucco
4 large beef or veal osso
    bucco (approximately
    1.25 kg/2 lb 12 oz)
sea salt and freshly ground
    black pepper
2 tablespoons grapeseed oil
4 carrots, sliced
1 large onion, roughly
    chopped
3 garlic cloves, sliced
250 ml (9 fl oz/1 cup) freshly
    squeezed orange juice
3 bay leaves
4 rosemary sprigs
400 g (14 oz) chopped
    tomatoes, tinned or fresh

Cauliflower purée
$\frac{1}{2}$ a large head cauliflower,
    roughly chopped
4 tablespoons olive oil
30 g (1 oz/$\frac{1}{3}$ cup) parmesan
    cheese (optional, for a non
    dairy-free version)

Preheat the oven to 160°C (315°F). Remove the osso bucco from the fridge 20 minutes prior to cooking to give it time to come to room temperature. Season the osso bucco generously on both sides with salt and pepper. Place a large flameproof casserole dish on the stove on a high heat and add a tablespoon of the grapeseed oil. (You can also use a large ovenproof frying pan for this step if you don't have an enamel pot.) Brown the osso bucco for approximately 6 minutes on each side, then transfer to a plate and set aside.

Add the remaining tablespoon of oil to the casserole dish and sauté the carrot, onion and garlic for 4–5 minutes, until the onion is translucent. Add the orange juice, bay leaves, rosemary and tomatoes, then bring everything to a simmer.

Add the osso bucco and spoon the liquids over the meat, then cover and cook in the oven for 4–5 hours.

While the meat is cooking, make the cauliflower purée by steaming the florettes for 6–8 minutes, or until tender. Once cooked, combine the cauliflower, olive oil, parmesan and 3 tablespoons of water with a good pinch of salt and pepper in a food processor and blitz until smooth. Taste and season again, if needed.

Warm the cauliflower purée in a small saucepan on the stove prior to serving.

Season the osso bucco well with salt and pepper and serve on a bed of cauliflower purée with the juices and vegetables from the pan spooned over the top.

SERVES 4

This cake is one of my favourite gluten-free treats of all time. It utilises every part of the orange (which is why I prefer organic oranges for this) to give a layered, zesty sweetness. I've used coconut sugar in place of caster (superfine) sugar and caramelised the oranges in maple syrup for a delicious sticky garnish. It's beautiful served with coconut yoghurt, whipped coconut cream, Greek-style yoghurt or quark.

Orange and almond cake

GF / DF / V

Cake

2 organic oranges

coconut oil, for greasing

6 eggs

280 g (10 oz/1⅔ cup) coconut sugar

225 g (8 oz/2¼ cups) almond meal

1 teaspoon aluminium- and gluten-free baking powder

Caramelised oranges

2 tablespoons maple syrup

2 organic oranges, peeled and sliced into 1 cm (½ inch) thick rounds

Serve with coconut yoghurt, whipped coconut cream, fresh passionfruit, Greek-style yoghurt or quark

To make the cake, bring a large saucepan of water to the boil. Wash the oranges well and add them to the pan, reduce the heat and simmer for 1½ hours. Once the time is up, remove the oranges from the pan and set aside to cool. Cut them open and remove any pips, then purée, peel and all, in a high-powered blender or food processor until the mixture is smooth, then set aside.

Preheat the oven to 160°C (315°F) and grease and line a 20 cm (8 inch) springform cake tin with baking paper.

Using an electric whisk, beat the eggs and sugar for 4–5 minutes until light in colour, then stir in the orange purée, almond meal and baking powder. Pour into the cake tin and bake for 1–1¼ hours, or

until the top is golden and a skewer inserted into the middle comes out clean. Allow to cool in the tin.

To make the caramelised oranges, heat the maple syrup in a sturdy large frying pan on a low heat. Add the orange slices and cook for approximately 3 minutes on each side, or until a lovely golden colour and caramelised. Remove the pan from the heat and allow to cool for a few minutes.

Remove the cake from the tin and top with the caramelised oranges. Serve with a dollop of whipped coconut cream, passionfruit, yoghurt or quark.

SERVES 8

Photograph page 10

Traditional macaroons include icing (confectioners') sugar, which makes them lighter in colour when cooked and also insanely sweet. I've used coconut sugar for mine as well as a mixed nut and seed meal (which is easy to find these days) to create a treat that hits all the same notes as one of my *pasticceria* favourites. You can also use a plain nut meal or a pure seed meal if that's all you have on hand. If these don't all go by the end of the lunch (and I think they probably will), they are good for up to a week in an airtight container.

LSA macaroons

GF / DF / V

2 egg whites
280 g (10 oz/1⅔ cup)
 coconut sugar
175 g (6 oz/1¼ cups)
 linseed, sunflower seed
 and almond meal
 (LSA mixture)
1 teaspoon vanilla extract
16 raw almonds,
 for decorating

Preheat the oven to 180°C (350°F) and line a baking tray (baking sheet) with baking paper.

Whisk the egg whites until firm peaks form, then gently fold through the remaining ingredients, except the almonds, using a large metal spoon to keep the air in the mixture.

Drop even tablespoonfuls of mixture onto the baking tray and top each one with an almond. Bake in the oven for 20 minutes, then turn the oven off and leave the door open with the macaroons inside for a further 10 minutes.

Remove from the oven and allow to cool completely on the tray before serving.

MAKES 16 MACAROONS

a country-style lunch

My family often travels south to my aunt's house in the country for special occasions. Her property is stunning and some of my fondest memories were created there. In the spring and summer when the fruit trees and flowers bloom and light up the garden, we'll run about picking flowers for the table and set up rugs in the sun for the kids to play on. In the autumn, the leaves on the fig trees change colours and cast an incredible golden glow over the grass. By winter, those leaves have fallen, leaving the trees bare, like beautiful skeletons. There's frost on the grass and the smell of wood fire in the air. We've had all sorts of family occasions throughout the seasons, celebrating in the garden or the cottage — always with plenty of delicious food. A winter lunch in the country is made for nourishing, hearty fare and a great bottle of wine. My family is always good for that.

SERVES 4

TO START

TOMATO AND
CARROT SOUP

MAINS

CHICKEN AND
LEEK PIE WITH A
CAULIFLOWER CRUST

SPICED LAMB RUMPS
WITH SALSA VERDE

SIDES

SPROUTING
GREENS SALAD

SIMPLE BAKED
CABBAGE

SWEET

ZUCCHINI LOAF

APPLE AND
PEAR CRUMBLE

TO DRINK

ALMOND MILK
HOT CHOCOLATE

Tomatoes and carrots are rich in antioxidants, in particular beta-carotenes and lycopene. Beta-carotenes are the building blocks of vitamin A, which is important for good vision and reducing inflammatory skin conditions such as eczema or acne. Consuming adequate amounts of lycopene has been shown to lower the risk of developing colon, breast, prostate, lung or skin cancers. It also decreases the risk of macular degeneration, which is responsible for loss of vision, and lowers the risk of developing heart disease. An awesome list of benefits!

Tomato and carrot soup

GF / DF OPTION / SF / V / VG OPTION

1 tablespoon coconut
   or grapeseed oil
1 large onion, roughly
   chopped
2 garlic cloves, sliced
4 large carrots, roughly
   chopped
1 x 400 g (14 oz) tin
   of chopped tomatoes,
   or fresh tomatoes
   (blanched, peeled,
   seeded and chopped)
750 ml (26 fl oz/3 cups)
   vegetable stock
½ teaspoon Celtic sea salt
freshly ground black
   pepper

Serve with chopped basil
   or oregano, Greek-style
   yoghurt and a few
   chopped baby tomatoes

Warm the oil in a saucepan on a medium heat. Once hot, add the onion, garlic and carrots. Cover with a lid and allow the vegetables to sweat for approximately 6–8 minutes, stirring occasionally. Add the tomatoes, stock, salt and a few grinds of pepper, then replace the lid and bring the soup to the boil. Immediately reduce the heat to a simmer and cook with the lid off for a further 45 minutes, so the flavours intensify as the soup reduces. Give it a stir every few minutes.

Take off the heat and allow to cool slightly before blitzing in a blender or food processor until smooth.

Gently reheat the soup, if required, before serving topped with a spoonful of yoghurt, chopped tomatoes and a sprinkling of herbs.

SERVES 4

Sprouting greens salad

GF / DF / SF / V / VG

Sprouts are nutritional powerhouses because they are seeds, grains or beans in the process of germinating, so the nutrients inside them are unlocked and made available to us when we eat them. To keep things quick and easy, I usually buy sprouts from the market for this salad, but you can also make your own at home over a two- to- three-day period by soaking and then draining the seed, grain or bean of your choice.

30 g (1 oz/½ cup) alfalfa sprouts
60 g (2¼ oz/½ cup) mung bean sprouts
2 spring onions (scallions), white parts only,
  finely sliced
1 zucchini (courgette), grated
1 Lebanese cucumber, roughly chopped
1½ handfuls of roughly chopped rocket
  (arugula) leaves
1 baby cos lettuce, leaves separated
a handful of mint leaves
a handful of coriander (cilantro) leaves

Dressing
2 tablespoons extra virgin olive oil
1 teaspoon dijon mustard
1 teaspoon apple cider vinegar

Combine all of the salad ingredients on a large serving platter and toss lightly.

Combine the dressing ingredients, drizzle over the salad and serve.

SERVES 4

Simple baked cabbage

GF / DF OPTION / SF / V / VG OPTION

Cabbage is another one of those underrated (and sometimes flat-out hated) vegetables. It's rich in sulphur-containing compounds, which support the body's natural detoxification pathways. I'll often bake it to eat as an accompaniment to a meal or to throw into salads or my 'nourish' bowls the following day. Nourish bowls are my delicious combos of whatever needs using up in my fridge. I like to give those ingredients a beauty makeover by putting them together with other vegetables, adding fresh herbs and a sprinkling of seeds, nuts or edible flowers. These bowls are always colourful and loaded with vegetables.

½ a red cabbage
2 tablespoons grapeseed or melted coconut oil
½ a lemon

Serve with some shaved parmesan (optional),
  wedges of lemon, some flat-leaf (Italian) parsley
  leaves and freshly ground black pepper

Preheat the oven to 200°C (400°F) and line a large baking tray (baking sheet) with baking paper.

Slice the cabbage into eight wedges, keeping the leaves together as much as possible.

Arrange the small wedges on the tray, drizzle over the oil and bake in the oven for 20 minutes, or until slightly crisped.

Serve with some shaved parmesan, if using, a squeeze of lemon juice and the parsley leaves and ground black pepper sprinkled on top.

SERVES 4

SPROUTING GREENS SALAD

I couldn't write a country menu that didn't include a pie or a crumble of some sort. Although my pies aren't 'traditional', I like to think they still create that beautiful warmth in your belly, just without the overly full sensation that often comes with pastry pies. I've used a cauliflower crust to finish this pie as I find it's convincingly creamy, like a potato mash, but much richer nutritionally. You could go with a different combo of root vegetables in your crust, or mix it with broccoli, if you like.

Chicken and leek pie with a cauliflower crust

GF / DF / SF

800 g (1 lb 12 oz)
   cauliflower
2 tablespoons olive oil
sea salt and freshly ground
   black pepper
2 tablespoons grapeseed oil
500 g (1 lb 2 oz) leeks, white
   parts only, thinly sliced
3 celery stalks, sliced
500 g (1 lb 2 oz) chicken
   breasts, cut into 2 cm
   ($\frac{3}{4}$ inch) dice
500 g (1 lb 2 oz) chicken
   thighs, cut into 2 cm
   ($\frac{3}{4}$ inch) dice
1 tablespoon thyme leaves
2 tablespoons finely
   chopped flat-leaf (Italian)
   parsley leaves
375 ml (13 fl oz/1$\frac{1}{2}$ cups)
   chicken stock
1 tablespoon cornflour
   (cornstarch), brown rice
   flour or ivory teff flour
1 egg, lightly beaten

Preheat the oven to 200°C (400°F). To make the cauliflower crust, steam the cauliflower florets until soft. Transfer to a food processor with the olive oil and a good pinch of salt and blitz until creamy. Set aside.

To make the pie filling, put 1 tablespoon of the grapeseed oil in a large frying pan over a medium heat. Add the leek and celery and sauté for 10 minutes, or until the leek has softened and is translucent. Transfer to a bowl.

Add the remaining tablespoon of grapeseed oil to the pan, then add the diced chicken and cook until just golden, but not entirely cooked. Return the leek and celery to the pan and add the thyme and parsley leaves. Toss everything together lightly, then transfer half of this mixture to a bowl. Add the stock to the pan and stir gently.

Put the cornflour in a small jug and mix in some of the stock from the pan. Stir to form a paste, then spoon this back into the pan, whisking as you go, and allow the stock to thicken. Return the chicken mixture in the bowl back to the pan and season well.

Pour the chicken filling into a 1.5 litre (52 fl oz/6 cup) capacity pie dish or ceramic lasagne dish and top with the cauliflower crust.

Brush the beaten egg all over the top then bake in the oven for 30 minutes until the crust is lovely and golden.

SERVES 4-6

Lamb rumps are one of the cheaper cuts of meat. They're also often accompanied with a considerable layer of fat. I trim most of this fat off prior to rubbing the lamb with the spice, and before tying and cooking it; this gives you a better flavour and a nicer-looking piece of meat to present at the table.

Spiced lamb rumps with salsa verde

GF / DF / SF   SALSA VERDE GF / DF / SF / V / VG

2 lamb rumps (approximately
    800 g/1 lb 12 oz in total),
    fat trimmed and gently
    tied with cotton twine
    (I hate to use synthetic
    string for cooking)
grapeseed oil, for frying

Spice rub
2 tablespoons ground
    coriander
1 tablespoon sesame seeds
$\frac{1}{2}$ teaspoon cayenne pepper
a pinch of sea salt

Salsa verde
45 g (1$\frac{3}{4}$ oz/1 cup) baby
    spinach leaves
125 ml (4 fl oz/$\frac{1}{2}$ cup)
    olive oil
a large handful of
    flat-leaf (Italian) parsley
    leaves
1 tablespoon grated
    horseradish, either fresh
    or from a jar
1 teaspoon apple cider vinegar
sea salt and freshly
    ground black pepper

Preheat the oven to 200°C (400°F). Combine the rub ingredients in a small bowl, then massage it into the lamb rumps, making sure all the flesh is well covered.

Heat a large ovenproof frying pan over a high heat and add a drop of grapeseed oil. Brown the rumps all over for approximately 10 minutes, turning every couple of minutes. Once browned, transfer the pan to the oven and cook for a further 20 minutes.

While the lamb is cooking, combine all of the salsa verde ingredients in a blender or food processor and blitz until smooth. (Any leftover salsa verde can be stored in a glass jar in the fridge for up to 1 week.)

Once cooked, allow the lamb to rest, covered with foil, for 5 minutes, then remove the cooking twine. Slice thickly and serve on a large platter with the salsa verde on the side, or drizzled over the top.

SERVES 4

Zucchini (courgettes) are a really versatile vegetable for both sweet and savoury foods. I use them raw in salads, turn them into noodles (see page 190), bake them, and grate them to pop into sweet treats and smoothies to sneak in an extra bit of plant power. In this loaf, the zucchini combines beautifully with the dried fruits to make a super-moist, gluten-free treat that is just delicious with a cuppa.

Zucchini loaf

DF / SF / V

125 ml (4 fl oz/$\frac{1}{2}$ cup) melted coconut oil

2 tablespoons maple syrup

3 eggs, beaten

1 teaspoon vanilla paste or extract

1 teaspoon ground cinnamon

$\frac{1}{2}$ teaspoon bicarbonate of soda (baking soda)

2 teaspoons aluminium- and gluten-free baking powder

2 zucchini (courgettes), grated

115 g (4 oz/$\frac{3}{4}$ cup) currants

125 g (4$\frac{1}{2}$ oz/$\frac{3}{4}$ cup) sultanas

60 g (2$\frac{1}{4}$ oz/$\frac{1}{2}$ cup) chopped pecans

65 g (2$\frac{1}{2}$ oz/1 cup) shredded coconut

110 g (3$\frac{3}{4}$ oz/1 cup) spelt flour

Preheat the oven to 180°C (350°F) and line a 12 × 22 cm (4$\frac{1}{2}$ × 8$\frac{1}{2}$ inch) loaf tin with baking paper.

Mix the coconut oil, maple syrup, eggs, vanilla, cinnamon, bicarbonate of soda and baking powder together in a large bowl until well combined. Add the zucchini, currants, sultanas and pecans and mix gently.

Fold in the coconut and spelt flours and combine all the ingredients together gently. Spoon into the loaf tin and bake for 45–55 minutes, or until a skewer inserted into the middle comes out clean.

SERVES 8

Apple and
pear crumble

DF OPTION / SF / V / VG

2 large green apples, skin on,
  cored and roughly chopped
2 ripe pears, skin on, cored and roughly chopped
1 tablespoon vanilla paste or extract
2 teaspoons ground cinnamon

Crumble
90 g (3¼ oz/¾ cup) spelt flour
75 g (2¾ oz/¾ cup) rolled oats
55 g (2 oz/¾ cup) shredded coconut
3 tablespoons maple syrup
3 tablespoons macadamia oil
  (or grapeseed oil or melted butter)
130 g (4¾ oz/½ cup) chopped raw mixed nuts

Serve with Greek-style or coconut yoghurt

Preheat the oven to 180°C (350°F). Put the apples
and pears in a 25 cm (10 inch) capacity pie dish
and add the vanilla, 3 tablespoons of water and
the cinnamon. Mix everything around, then bake
in the oven for 20 minutes.

Combine the crumble ingredients in a mixing
bowl, then remove the pie dish of fruit from the
oven and spread the crumble mixture all over the
top. Return to the oven to cook for approximately
30–40 minutes, or until the crumble is lightly
golden and crispy.

Serve with a generous dollop of Greek-style or
coconut yoghurt.

SERVES 8

Almond milk
hot chocolate

GF / DF / SF / V / VG

When you mix slippery elm powder into
your food or drink, it thickens and becomes
slightly gel-like. These are some of the
beautiful properties of the slippery elm
coming to life. This gel coats and soothes
the mouth, throat and intestines. Needless
to say it works a treat whisked into warmed
milk and adds some digestive support to
this delicious dairy-free hot chocolate.

1 litre (35 fl oz/4 cups) unsweetened almond milk
40 g (1½ oz/⅓ cup) raw cacao powder
1½ teaspoons ground cinnamon
2 teaspoons slippery elm powder
3 tablespoons rice malt syrup

Combine all of the ingredients in a small saucepan
and whisk over a low heat for approximately
6 minutes to ensure the powders are dissolved
into the milk and the mixture is nice and hot.
Pour into cups and serve.

SERVES 4

Christmas ... anytime!

It's all too common these days to have family or friends living in far-away places, so having a big family Christmas isn't always possible. But I see this as a great excuse to celebrate Christmas with the ones you love, whenever you are able to seize the opportunity to be together, festive season or not!

Christmas is exciting, buzzing, nurturing and insanely fun. I love the care that's put into planning a Christmas menu and the intimacy shared by everyone at the table.

A Christmas menu should always provide a beautiful balance of food. A slow start with deliciously extravagant nibbles, seafood to break in the meal and a beautiful main shared between all is how my family likes to play it. And when it comes to dessert, well, the spice of a Christmas fruitcake, retro appeal of a trifle and a few gingerbread cookies are all you need to top off the experience.

SERVES 4

APPETISERS
CHICKEN LIVER PÂTÉ

CASHEW CHEESE WITH TRUFFLE OIL

ENTRÉE
SEAFOOD BOUILLABAISSE

MAIN
SLOW-ROASTED PORK SHOULDER

SIDES
ROASTED BABY CARROTS WITH CRISPY KALE AND ZA'ATAR

BAKED LEEKS

SUPERFOOD SALAD

SILVERBEET, LENTIL, GOAT'S CHEESE AND APPLE SALAD

DESSERTS
GINGERBREAD STARS

BERRY CUSTARD PARFAIT

SPELT FRUITCAKE

Chicken liver pâté

GF / SF

Liver is a great source of vitamin A and iron. It's my preference to seek out organic chicken livers because the liver's job is to clean the bloodstream, detoxify the system and store energy. So if you're going to eat liver (and you should — it's delicious), it's nice to know the animal lived as good a life as possible.

2 tablespoons grapeseed oil
1 small onion, finely chopped
2 garlic cloves, finely chopped
400 g (14 oz) organic chicken livers
a pinch of ground cinnamon
a pinch of ground cloves
a few grinds of freshly ground black pepper
   and a pinch of sea salt
2 tablespoons finely chopped chives
125 ml (4 fl oz/½ cup) chicken stock
150 g (5½ oz) butter, softened

Heat 1 tablespoon of the oil in a frying pan over a low heat. Add the onion and garlic, and sauté for 5–8 minutes, or until the onion has softened and is translucent. Remove from the pan and set aside.

Wipe the pan clean with paper towels, then heat the remaining tablespoon of oil over a medium heat. Add the chicken livers and cook for 2 minutes on each side. Add the spices, chives and stock and reduce the liquid mixture for about 3 minutes. Remove from the pan and allow to cool.

Blend all the ingredients in a food processor, including the butter, until smooth. Transfer to serving bowls or ramekins, cover with plastic wrap and refrigerate until needed. Serve garnished with chopped herbs, if you like.

MAKES 400 G (14 OZ) (ENOUGH TO SERVE 4–6)

Cashew cheese with truffle oil

GF / DF / SF / V / VG

Cashew cheese is a scrumptious vegan substitute for dairy cheese. Once blended with the other ingredients in this recipe, the soaked cashews create a lovely cream-cheese-like consistency. I've used truffle oil to add more depth to the flavour, but it's also heavenly with fresh herbs or simply as is.

155 g (5½ oz/1 cup) raw cashews, soaked for one hour
3 tablespoons filtered water
2 tablespoons nutritional yeast
2 teaspoons apple cider vinegar
2 tablespoons lemon juice
½ a garlic clove
2 tablespoons truffle oil
sea salt and freshly ground black pepper

Combine all of the ingredients in the bowl of a food processor and blend until creamy. Transfer to whichever serving bowls you plan on using, then cover and refrigerate until needed, or serve straight away.

The cashew cheese will keep in an airtight container in the fridge for 4 days. I like to serve a big scoop of this on a plate with nice crackers or veggies.

MAKES 400 G (14 OZ)

I remember trying bouillabaisse as a youngster when Dad made it, and I've loved it ever since. Given that, I don't think I could possibly write a book without featuring it somewhere. It's beautiful when flavours ignite memories, and this recipe does just that for me.

Seafood bouillabaisse

GF / DF / SF

2 tablespoons grapeseed oil
3 garlic cloves, sliced
2 celery stalks, diced
1 x 400 g (14 oz) tin
    of chopped tomatoes
    (or fresh, blanched,
    peeled and diced)
375 ml (13 fl oz/1½ cups)
    fish stock
1 tablespoon thyme leaves
375 g (13 oz) firm white fish
    (ling, cod and dory all
    work well)
8 raw king prawns,
    unpeeled
12 mussels, scrubbed
    clean and debearded
    (see method on page 212)
1 calamari/squid tube,
    cut into 6 rings

Serve with lemon wedges
    and freshly ground
    black pepper

Warm the oil in a large saucepan or a flameproof casserole dish on a medium heat. Add the garlic and celery and sauté for 2–3 minutes, or until translucent. Add the tomatoes, fish stock and thyme and bring slowly to the boil.

Arrange the fish and seafood in the dish to ensure everything is covered by liquid, then put the lid on and cook for approximately 8 minutes to ensure all of the seafood is cooked. Discard any mussels that haven't opened.

Serve straight from the dish at the table, or divide between serving bowls and serve with lemon wedges on the side and a good grind of black pepper.

SERVES 4

I was lucky enough to feast on this deliciously melty pork one Mother's Day at a stunning macadamia nut farm, and this recipe is courtesy of my lovely friend, the host on that day. It is a truly wonderful, melt-in-your-mouth dish. The slow-cooking results in pork that is deeply flavoured and just incredible to eat. In the colder months, I like to serve this with warm baked apples or pear chutney (see page 174). In summer, it works beautifully with fresh mango chutney.

Slow-roasted pork shoulder

GF / DF

1.6 kg (3 lb 8 oz) shoulder of pork from the neck end, bone in
1 tablespoon Himalayan salt
2 tablespoons coconut sugar
1 tablespoon smoked paprika

Take the pork out of the fridge at least an hour before cooking to come to room temperature. Score the skin carefully (see page 174 for my tips on how to achieve great crackling). Preheat the oven to 220°C (425°F).

Pat the pork dry with paper towel and put it in a large roasting tin. Combine the salt, sugar and paprika and rub this mixture all over the pork, making sure it is well covered.

Put the pork in the oven and roast for about 40 minutes, then remove from the oven and reduce the temperature to 125°C (240°F). Cover the roasting tray tightly with a double layer of foil, then return the pork to the oven and cook for about 6–7 hours, or until the internal temperature measures 89°C (192°F) and the meat is soft enough to pull apart with a spoon.

Pour off and reserve the pan juices. Increase the temperature back up to 220°C and cook the pork, uncovered, for 10 minutes so it becomes slightly crispy. Remove from the oven, cover and allow to rest for 30 minutes.

Using two forks, pull the meat away from the bone, cut the crackling into small pieces and arrange the meat and the crackling on a platter. Pour any juices from the pan over the pork and serve.

SERVES 6-8

SLOW-ROASTED PORK SHOULDER

ROASTED BABY CARROTS WITH
CRISPY KALE AND ZA'ATAR
recipe page 240

Roasted baby carrots with crispy kale and za'atar

GF / DF / SF / V / VG

Za'atar is a Middle Eastern spice blend that combines thyme, sesame seeds, sea salt and sumac — and it's completely delicious, especially with these carrots. If you don't have za'atar, simply sprinkle the salad with sesame seeds, sea salt and some of your favourite dried herbs.

4 large kale leaves, stalks discarded,
  leaves roughly torn into large pieces
1 bunch of baby carrots (approximately
  185 g/6½ oz)
1 tablespoon coconut oil, melted
1 tablespoon za'atar

Preheat the oven to 160°C (315°F) and line a large baking tray (baking sheet) with baking paper.

Place the torn kale leaves and baby carrots in a large bowl and toss with the melted coconut oil. Spread the carrots around one end of the baking tray and the kale around the other, so the juices from the carrots don't prevent the kale leaves from crisping up. Roast for 25 minutes.

Once cooked, slice the carrots lengthways and toss them with za'atar. Arrange the kale and carrots on a platter and serve.

SERVES 4

Photographs pages 239 & 242

Baked leeks

GF / DF / SF / V / VG

4 leeks, washed and green ends discarded
2 tablespoons grapeseed or olive oil
1 teaspoon (dried or fresh) thyme leaves
1 teaspoon (dried or fresh) oregano leaves
sea salt and freshly ground black pepper

Preheat the oven to 200°C (400°F) and line a baking tray (baking sheet) with baking paper.

Drop the leeks into a bowl of boiling water to blanch them for 4–5 minutes. Remove, drain on paper towels, then cut them into quarters lengthways and arrange on the baking tray. Drizzle with the oil, scatter over the thyme and oregano and season with salt. Bake for 20 minutes until they are starting to look caramelised.

Once you are happy, remove them from the oven, transfer to a serving plate, give them a good grinding of pepper and serve immediately.

SERVES 4

When you serve kale raw in a salad it's really important to marinate it first by massaging it with lemon and salt. This tenderises the otherwise quite fibrous leaves, making them really delicious.

Superfood salad

GF / DF OPTION / SF / V / VG OPTION

1 large beetroot (beet),
   washed and top discarded
3 kale leaves, stalks discarded,
   leaves roughly torn
juice of $\frac{1}{2}$ a lemon
a pinch of sea salt
1 small red capsicum (pepper),
   seeded and roughly chopped
1 large sweet potato,
   roughly chopped
1 tablespoon coconut oil, melted
140 g (5 oz/1 cup) cherry
   tomatoes, halved
$\frac{1}{2}$ an avocado, diced
a small handful of basil
   leaves, torn
a small handful of flat-leaf
   (Italian) parsley leaves
1 tablespoon chia seeds
2 teaspoons white sesame seeds
freshly ground black pepper
Optional: walnuts and feta or
   goat's cheese for sprinkling
   over the salad

Dressing
2 tablespoons extra virgin
   olive oil
1 teaspoon apple cider vinegar
1 teaspoon yellow mustard seeds

Preheat the oven to 200°C (400°F), wrap the beetroot in foil and bake for 45 minutes.

While the beetroot is cooking, put the torn kale leaves into a large bowl, pour over the lemon juice and sprinkle with salt, then, using clean hands, massage the lemon and salt into the kale for approximately 5 minutes. Set aside.

Line a baking tray (baking sheet) with baking paper. Spread the capsicum and sweet potato around the baking tray, drizzle with the coconut oil, then place in the oven with the beetroot. Cook for 20 minutes, then remove all the vegetables from the oven.

Allow the vegetables to cool for approximately 10 minutes. Peel the skin from the beetroot (use gloves if you don't want red hands). Trim the ends, then cut the beetroot into eighths. Remove the skin from the capsicum pieces, if you like.

Combine all the dressing ingredients in a small jar and shake well.

Divide the kale leaves, roasted vegetables, cherry tomatoes, avocado and herbs between two serving plates, sprinkle with chia and sesame seeds and finish with the dressing and a good grind of pepper.

SERVES 4

This is a really textured and nutritious salad. Lentils are a great way to up the plant protein in a meal. Both brown or puy (French) lentils will taste sensational here. Not much else is required to highlight the other flavours in this salad, they all shine and complement each other beautifully.

Silverbeet, lentil, goat's cheese and apple salad

GF / SF / V

1 small green apple, cored and finely grated or julienned
2 tablespoons lemon juice (approximately 1 lemon)
4 large silverbeet (Swiss chard) leaves, stalks discarded and leaves shredded
70 g (2$\frac{1}{2}$ oz/$\frac{1}{2}$ cup) walnuts
200 g (7 oz/$\frac{3}{4}$ cup) cooked lentils (brown or puy)
35 g (1$\frac{1}{4}$ oz/$\frac{1}{4}$ cup) currants
80 g (2$\frac{3}{4}$ oz) goat's cheese

Combine the apple and lemon juice in a small bowl and toss so the apple is coated in the juice.

Place the silverbeet, walnuts, lentils, currants and lemony apple in a large mixing bowl and toss together.

To serve, place half of the salad on a platter, crumble over half of the goat's cheese, then repeat with another layer of salad and cheese.

SERVES 4

Gingerbread and Christmas are like bread and butter: they just go together! These are such a cute way to be festive, and they are perfect with a cup of tea after lunch, or to pack up and send home with your guests as a special treat — in a brown paper bag, of course!

Gingerbread stars

V

520 g (1 lb 2½ oz/4½ cups)
    spelt flour
1 tablespoon ground ginger
1 teaspoon mixed spice
1 teaspoon bicarbonate
    of soda (baking soda)
150 g (5½ oz) unsalted
    butter, softened
100 g (3½ oz) coconut sugar
175 g (6 oz/½ cup) molasses
1 egg yolk, beaten

Combine the spelt flour, ginger, mixed spice and bicarbonate of soda in a large mixing bowl.

In another bowl, beat together the butter, coconut sugar, molasses and egg yolk until the mixture is smooth and free of lumps. This can be done by hand, or using a food processor or electric mixer.

Stir the wet mixture gradually through the dry ingredients to form a sticky dough. Place in an oiled bowl, cover with plastic wrap or a tea towel and place in the fridge for approximately 1 hour to allow the dough to firm up.

Once the dough is chilled, preheat the oven to 160°C (315°F). Line two baking trays (baking sheets) with baking paper. Place the cold dough between two large

sheets of baking paper. Using a rolling pin, roll out the dough until it is around 3 mm (⅛ inch) thick. Remove the top layer of baking paper and cut the dough into stars using a cookie cutter. Transfer these stars to the lined baking trays and bake for 10 minutes, or until lightly golden.

Remove from the oven and allow to cool on the baking tray for another 10 minutes, then serve as they are, or decorate with drizzles of melted dark chocolate. They keep well in an airtight container for about 5 days.

**MAKES ABOUT 20 STARS
(DEPENDING ON THE SIZE
OF YOUR COOKIE CUTTER)**

My berry parfait might be a bit retro, but there are a few members of the family who don't consider a Christmas meal complete without a parfait or trifle of some sort on the table. So this one's for them. It's an oldie that I've updated with new-style ingredients that I love. Bet everyone will love it just as much, if not more, than the creamy, sugary parfaits of their youth.

Berry custard parfait

GF / DF / V

Berry purée
2 cups of seasonal berries
1 tablespoon acai powder
1 teaspoon camu powder

Coconut and macadamia crumble
40 g (1½ oz/¼ cup) macadamia nuts
35 g (1¼ oz/¼ cup) pistachios
30 g (1 oz/½ cup) coconut flakes

Custard
500 ml (17 fl oz/2 cups) coconut milk
4 tablespoons coconut nectar or coconut sugar
2 teaspoons vanilla extract or ½ a vanilla bean, split and seeds scraped
6 egg yolks, beaten
1 tablespoon gluten-free cornflour (cornstarch) or 2 tablespoons brown rice flour

Place all the ingredients for the berry purée in a blender and blitz until smooth.

To make the crumble topping, preheat the oven to 180°C (350°F) and line a large baking tray (baking sheet) with baking paper. Toast the nuts and coconut flakes gently in the oven for 10 minutes until lightly golden. Once cooked, set aside.

Meanwhile, make the custard by combining the coconut milk, coconut nectar or sugar and vanilla in a small saucepan (off the heat) and whisking together. Place over a low heat, add the egg yolks and keep stirring while the custard warms — this may take some time, but it's an important step. The heat must be kept low and you must stir continuously, otherwise you may end up with scrambled eggs.

Put the cornflour in a small jug and add a little of the custard mixture. Stir well to form a paste, then pour this paste back into the saucepan and whisk it into the mixture. Keep whisking while the mixture thickens. Just as it starts coming to the boil, remove from the heat and allow to cool slightly before serving.

To finish, take jars, bowls or shallow wine or cocktail glasses and spoon layers of the custard, berry purée and crumble into each one, layering each twice over. Refrigerate until needed and serve chilled.

SERVES 4

I have a complete love affair with fruitcake. I make several every Christmas to give to friends and one, of course, for my own family. They are always so well received. Generally, recipes for fruitcake involve candied fruits and alcohol, neither of which I like to include in mine, so I'm bringing zing and moisture to the recipe through pure fruit zests and juice.

Spelt fruitcake

GF / V

720 g (1 lb 9 oz) currants
200 g (7 oz) raisins
125 ml (4 fl oz/½ cup) freshly squeezed orange juice (about 1 big orange)
1 teaspoon finely grated orange zest
1 teaspoon finely grated lemon zest
1 teaspoon mixed allspice
1 teaspoon ground cinnamon
½ teaspoon ground nutmeg
180 g (6¼ oz) butter, softened
130 g (4¾ oz/⅔ cup) coconut sugar
5 eggs, beaten
300 g (10½ oz/2 cups) spelt flour
a good pinch of sea salt
30 g (1 oz/¼ cup) blanched almonds

Preheat the oven to 160°C (315°F) and triple-line a 20 cm (8 inch) square or round cake tin with baking paper.

Combine the currants, raisins, orange juice, orange and lemon zests and spices in a bowl.

Put the butter in a separate large mixing bowl and beat using a handheld electric mixer (or a wooden spoon if necessary) until light and creamy. Add the coconut sugar and beat well, followed by the eggs, adding in increments and beating well after each addition. Add the dry fruit mix to the butter mixture in large spoonfuls, then fold to combine. Fold in the spelt flour and salt until well combined.

Pour the batter into the lined tin and arrange the blanched almonds on top in a flower pattern. Place an additional piece of baking paper over the top of the cake so it hangs over the edge of the tin, and use cooking twine to tie the baking paper down around the top of the cake tin. This will stop the top of the cake from burning. Place in the middle of the oven and cook for 2½–3 hours. Leave in the tin until the cake has completely cooled.

The cake can be stored for up to 3 weeks in an airtight container in a cool, dark place.

MAKES 1 CAKE, WHICH YIELDS 16 SLICES

index

acknowledgements

This book has long been a dream of mine, and it could not have come together without the incredible support of so many magnificent people around me. To my wonderful publisher, Diana Hill at Murdoch Books — when you first asked if I had ever considered writing a book, I gasped, smiled, cried, then turned the music up loud and danced around the room with Jet. It was an incredible moment in my life and I am humbled that you looked at what I love to do, in my work and my life, and put all the forces in place to create something so beautiful to share with the world. Thank you. To the insane team at Murdoch, who have taught, guided and encouraged me so beautifully in this process: Katie Bosher, Megan Pigott, Madeleine Kane and Alexandra Gonzalez — thank you. My dream book couldn't have been created so seamlessly without your expertise, creativity, knowledge and wonderful spirits. Thank you for your patience, wisdom and energy. Special thanks as well to Wendy Quisumbing and Katy Holder for all their amazing work. To the dream creative team: Jason Loucas and Vanessa Austin, thank you for bringing my vision in celebrating nutrition, health and food to life in such a fun, inspiring and exciting way. I have learned so much from you both on this journey and will carry all these things with me in the years to come. You are true artists and I am so honoured to have worked with you. To all the lovely people who turned up at my little market stall in Bondi when The Brown Paper Bag first began, thank you for your encouragement and feedback. Because of you, The Brown Paper Bag grew and I gained the confidence to turn my ideas into a book. To my clients and colleagues, I thank you. It is because we connect that new ideas are born. I have learned so much from you and my understanding of people, nutrition, food and life has evolved because of that. To my gorgeous girls, Sarina and Vic, who worked tirelessly with me in The Brown Paper Bag kitchen, you laugh at me when I jump about with ideas, keep me focused on what

needs to be done and provide endless support to the business, the book and to me personally. I'm grateful such beautiful women as you have walked into my life. I thank you always. To a true believer in my work, Jess Blanch. You picked up a little flyer with my handcrafted business logo early on and invited me to open my creative channels through writing. May you always know how much this built my confidence. I write from my heart always and your guidance since those very early days gives me the ability to be this way. Thank you.

To my greatest foodie inspiration, Jody Vassallo. When I was 15 years old doing work experience (at Murdoch, of all places!), I picked up a cookbook full of your beautiful work. I fell in love with everything about it and thought 'one day I want to write one, too.' You are uniquely creative, and amazingly talented and I am inspired by your work. I'm honoured to call you a friend for life.

To my friends, old and new, some who feature in this book: Elisa, Paul, Katie, Lauren and Sally, thank you all for being a part of my life. Your gentle footprints are in my heart.

To my family: Mum, Dad, Dini, Romy, Russ, Rich, Marg, Milla, Hudson, Anais and Tatum. You are my grounding force, inspiration, honest critics and the ultimate believers. I wouldn't be where I am now without you. I am forever grateful for all you do to support me, for the values you have instilled in me and for your love.

Finally, to my son, Jet. Darling boy, one day when you read this, I want you to know what a blessing you are to me. When you came into my world, everything changed, and I truly began creating a dream life; one that is always a celebration and bursting with love. I am grateful for the happiness and love we share and thank you for everything you have taught me, for your smiles, your giggles, your patience, your happiness and your incredible soul, my beautiful boy. I love you with all that I am and more. *Jacqueline x*

Published in 2016 by Murdoch Books, an imprint of Allen & Unwin

Murdoch Books Australia
83 Alexander Street
Crows Nest NSW 2065
Phone: +61 (0) 2 8425 0100
murdochbooks.com.au
info@murdochbooks.com.au

Murdoch Books UK
Ormond House
26–27 Boswell Street
London, WC1N 3JZ
Phone: +44 (0) 20 8785 5995
murdochbooks.co.uk
info@murdochbooks.co.uk

For Corporate Orders & Custom Publishing contact Noel Hammond,
National Business Development Manager, Murdoch Books Australia

Publisher: Diana Hill
Editorial Manager: Katie Bosher
Design Manager: Megan Pigott
Designer: Madeleine Kane
Photographer: Jason Loucas
Stylist: Vanessa Austin
Food Editor: Katy Holder
Home Economist: Wendy Quisumbing
Production Manager: Alexandra Gonzalez

A cataloguing-in-publication entry is available from the catalogue
of the National Library of Australia at nla.gov.au.

ISBN 978 1 74336 704 9 Australia
ISBN 978 1 74336 748 3 UK

A catalogue record for this book is available from the British Library.

Colour reproduction by Splitting Image Colour Studio Pty Ltd,
Clayton, Victoria
Printed by 1010 Printing International Limited, China

The author wishes to thank the following companies and individuals
for the loan of their beautiful products, which appear in the
photographs in this book: Brett Stone (represented by Utopia
Galleries), Black Sun Creative Arts, Cherie Peyton, Chu Chu,
Claypool, Dulux, Emily Ziz, Jemima Woo, Kim Wallace Ceramics,
Little White Dish, Mud Australia, Robert Gordon and Wedgwood.

IMPORTANT: Those who might be
at risk from the effects of salmonella
poisoning (the elderly, pregnant women,
young children and those suffering
from immune deficiency diseases)
should consult their doctor with any
concerns about eating raw eggs.

OVEN GUIDE: You may find cooking
times vary depending on the oven you
are using. For fan-forced ovens, as a
general rule, set the oven temperature
to 20°C (35°F) lower than indicated
in the recipe.

MEASURES GUIDE: We have used
20 ml (4 teaspoon) tablespoon
measures. If you are using a 15 ml
(3 teaspoon) tablespoon add an extra
teaspoon of the ingredient for each
tablespoon specified.